INTERNATIONAL PERCEPTIONS OF THE SUPERPOWER MILITARY BALANCE

edited by
Donald C. Daniel

PRAEGER PUBLISHERS
Praeger Special Studies

48300

New York　　•　　London　　•　　Sydney　　•　　Toronto

Library of Congress Cataloging in Publication Data

Main entry under title:

International perceptions of the superpower
  military balance.

  Includes bibliographical references and index.
  1.   United States--Foreign relations--Russia.
2.   Russia--Foreign relations--United States.
3.   Balance of power. 4. Military policy.
I. Daniel, Donald C. F.
JX1428.R8I57   1978   355.03'3073   78-19456
ISBN 0-03-046471-4

PRAEGER PUBLISHERS
PRAEGER SPECIAL STUDIES
383 Madison Avenue, New York, N.Y. 10017, U.S.A.

Published in the United States of America in 1978
by Praeger Publishers,
A Division of Holt, Rinehart and Winston, CBS, Inc.

89   038   987654321

INTERNATIONAL PERCEPTIONS OF THE SUPERPOWER MILITARY BALANCE

PREFACE

On December 9, 1977, a meeting was held under the auspices of the Department of National Security Affairs of the Naval Postgraduate School in Monterey, California. The topic was "Perceptions of the U. S. -Soviet Military Balances," and, with the exception of Chapter Four, the papers grouped together in this book were presented at that meeting. Some were originally sponsored by the Director of Net Assessment, Office of the U. S. Secretary of Defense, and funded by the Defense Advanced Research Projects Agency.

This writer is pleased to acknowledge the support of Mr. Andrew W. Marshall, Director of Net Assessment of OSD; Admiral Noel Gayler, former commander-in-chief, U. S. Pacific forces; Professor Lawrence Caldwell of Occidental College; Mr. Derek Leebeart of The Program for Science and International Affairs, Harvard University; and a number of individuals at the Naval Postgraduate School. These include Rear Admiral Isham Linder, Superintendent; Dr. Robert R. Fossum, former Dean of Research; the members of the Research Council; and Professor Patrick J. Parker, Chairman of the Department of National Security Affairs. Chapter Four originally appeared in the Fall 1977 issue of International Security, and I wish to thank the President and Fellows of Harvard College for reprint permission.

Donald C. Daniel

CONTENTS

48300

LIST OF TABLES AND FIGURES

INTRODUCTION

Readers of international relations or "deterrence" literature are familiar with the proposition that the "actual amount" of power available to a state may not be as important in peacetime as its perceived military capability. If a state is viewed as being strong, then those views—and not its "true" military strength—may be decisive for reassuring allies and deterring foes. Conversely, if a state is accepted as weak or weakening, then allies may become nervous and foes more bold.

American policy makers have recently shown renewed interest in the significance of perceived power. Secretary of Defense Schlesinger, for example, writing about the strategic nuclear balance in his last Annual Defense Department Report, called upon the United States to "maintain capabilities such that everyone—friend, foe, and domestic audience alike—will perceive that we are the equal of our strongest competitors. We should not take the chance that, in this most hazardous of areas, misperceptions could lead to miscalculation, confrontation, and crisis."[1]

He stressed this theme again when writing about the naval balance: . . . the naval forces of the Soviet Union and its allies are not generally superior to those of the United States and its allies, and . . . this should be perceived by well-informed observers.[2]

This book accepts that perceptions are important in peacetime and that perceptions of U.S.-Soviet power are particularly worthy of investigation. It aims to make a contribution in two areas: (1) helping systematize the research field centering on these perceptions, and (2) offering empirically-based conclusions as to the comparative ranking of the superpowers in perceived strength, the factors which condition those views, and the policy consequences flowing from them in the minds of perceivers.

Part I is devoted to analytical, methodological, and overall policy considerations. The first chapter presents a "general map" of the research field as it raises and organizes questions and problems faced by an analyst. The second chapter provides the rationale for arguing that U.S. policy makers should more consciously consider the perceptions impact of force development and deployment decisions, and the third recommends a procedure which builds upon the perceptions of experts to measure where countries stand in specific weapons systems balances.

Part II is substantive in nature, and its six chapters illustrate the use of different research methods and sources. The focus is on U. S. Soviet, British, French, German, Japanese, and Arab views of various superpower balances with overall military and strategic capabilities most often being the objects of their views.

Part III has only one chapter. It highlights and draws together some of the findings presented in part II.

There are many books which describe the military capabilities of the United States and the Soviet Union, but there are few which deal with how those capabilities are perceived. If any part of this book stimulates the reader to push further and develop more so-phisticated research techniques or to contribute to a cumulative base of evidence, then it will have served its purpose.

NOTES

1. James R. Schlesinger, Annual Defense Department Report, FY76 and FY197T (Washington: U. S. Government Printing Office, 1975), pp. I-14, I-21.

2. Ibid.

PART
1

RESEARCH AND OVERALL POLICY CONSIDERATIONS

1

PERCEPTIONS OF THE U.S.-SOVIET BALANCE: PROBLEMS OF ANALYSIS AND RESEARCH

Herbert Goldhamer

INTRODUCTION

This chapter outlines some of the analytical and practical problems involved in work on perceptions of the U. S. - USSR military balance. Since the aim is to raise and systematize questions and problems, the study is singularly abstract and dateless. Like a blank check, its utility depends on being filled in, and, of course, this is the objective of ongoing empirical work. A general map of the area may seem a dispensable luxury; however, as interest and work grow, some systemization of the field is useful to bring order and economy into research programs.

SOME CHARACTERISTICS OF PERCEPTIONS

Let us begin by clarifying certain nonsubstantive characteristics of perceptions of the military balance.

"Perception," in the present context, is used in a figurative sense. Technically, "percepts" and "perceptions" are central elaborations of sensory inputs. "Perceptions" of the U. S. - USSR balance result from reading or hearing something, but the sensory or perceptual input simply plays the role of a medium and is not the object of attention. A line in a newspaper is perceived, but its meaning is not a percept. In short, "perception" of the military balance could just as well be called "beliefs," "ideas," "impressions," or "convictions," depending on the nuance one wished to convey. This excursion into semantics probably should be unnecessary, but the suggestion that psychological theories of perception provide a

useful background for analysis of perceptions of the military balance
is, in my view, misleading. It transforms a figurative use of "perception" into a literal or technical use. This area of study could equally
well be called "Beliefs About the Military Balance." Presumably,
the "Psychology of Perception" would then be displaced by the
"Psychology of Belief." This certainly would be more appropriate.

"Perception" of military power makes more literal sense in
those cases where observers are at a military review or military
maneuvers or are present on a battlefield or at a naval or air
demonstration. Indeed, interesting substantive questions revolve
precisely around physical, visible military demonstrations and
concern the differential impact of a statement about military power
and a physical perception of it. The substantial impact that a physical
demonstration of a weapon often has results, no doubt, from the fact
that this is a perception in the technical sense and not just a statement. Evidently, however, in most contexts in which one speaks of
perceptions of military power, "perception of" is a figurative
substitute for "beliefs about."

Any attempt to convey perceptions of the U. S. -USSR balance
(either by the perceiver to an investigator or by the investigator to
his readers) runs the danger of giving the description greater exact-
ness and sharpness of contour than existed in the original perception.
The exigencies of exposition and communication put a premium on
reducing fuzziness or vagueness that may have existed in the original
perception. In fact, this vagueness may be a more important characteristic of the perception than its substantive content. What is
often required is an exact description of confusion. Confusion may
lend itself to manipulation much more readily than precise and well-
ordered knowledge and may provide a richer field, both in crises
and in stable situations, for the political use of military forces.

The question, What is the U. S. -USSR, strategic, NATO or
naval balance?, evokes an image of a balance and a needle moving along
a scale, and thus implies a quantitative answer in a single dimension,
or, more briefly, a single number. Obviously, of course, perceptions
of U. S. -USSR military power (even in a single sector—strategic, naval,
etc.) may be more complex than this. The better informed observers
are, the more their perceptions of U. S. and Soviet military power
are likely to be expressed by a set of statements not always reducible
to a few summary propositions. That a person may agree with one
or more propositions about the balance does not necessarily mean
that they are an adequate account of the perception of the balance.

The breadth or narrowness of an individual's perception of the
military balance may vary according to the amount of information
available; it may also result from varying conceptions of what is

relevant to an appreciation of the U. S. -USSR strategic, NATO, or naval balance.

Accounts of perceptions of the U. S. -USSR military balance should indicate, where at all possible, their degree of stability. This is particularly important in investigating the impact of a particular event on beliefs. Whether the effect endures for a day, a week, a month, or longer, is obviously of capital importance. Our interest in the stability of opinions will vary according to whether we are dealing with a crisis situation, a slowly evolving situation, or a quite stable international context. In crisis situations, knowledge of another's perception of the balance may be important even though the perception may change radically during the course of the crisis or have little enduring effect after it. Both the special interest attaching to perceptions during a crisis and the difficulty that may exist in studying them at that time raise questions concerning the feasibility of predicting changes in perception during crises from their precrisis status. Whether long-term swings in the perception of the military balance are the product of relatively stable perceptions undergoing slow evolution or are the product of a series of sharp shocks to beliefs, is an empirical question of considerable theoretical and practical interest. The stability or instability of perceptions has, of course, to be related to the stability or instability of the underlying reality.

Instability of perceptions are not necessarily related to changing political or military environments. Perception changes may represent instability in the data-gathering process, but they may also—and, of course, it is this that interests us—reflect a low level of attention, conviction, and clarity in the views of the people we are interviewing or observing. An elicited description of perceptions is sometimes a casual and unstable expression invented to provide an answer.

Perceptions of the military balance should be distinguished by the degree of confidence attached to them by the perceiver. Persons whose perceptions show considerable instability may nonetheless attach a high measure of confidence to them. The confidence or lack of confidence that the perceiver has in his perceptions may affect attention to, and absorption of, information on the balance.

Generally, we do not include, in speaking about perceptions of the military balance, any emotion or affect attached to these beliefs; that is, we treat the perception of the balance as purely cognitive and not as an affective event. The degree of confidence that people have in their perceptions already moves us into areas that are not purely cognitive. Perception of the military balance may be accompanied in varying degrees by fear, pride, anger, or other affects. These aspects of the perception may not always be easy to observe, but they must be presumed to affect the character of present and future perceptions.

We often think of perceptions of the military balance as representing comparisons of capabilities at a given moment. In fact, when we examine newspaper and journal materials, we find that much of what is written about the balance of military power deals with who is gaining on whom. Thus, an important component of perceptions of the military balance is the direction and rate of change in military capabilities. If one is behind, it is useful to emphasize a greater rate of growth, and this, of course, is what the Soviets have done in making economic comparisons between themselves and the United States. In the military field, they were not inclined to use this type of presentation in the past since they did not like to acknowledge their great inferiority in strategic and naval capabilities. U. S. spokesmen, on the other hand, have been very free in providing statements concerning the Soviet Union's catching up with the United States or surpassing it, so that a good deal of U. S. and world discussion has been in terms of rates of change. In any event, perception of the military balance may, for many perceivers, be essentially (a) a perception of impending changes in the balance, and (b) an imputation of superiority to the side with the greatest growth rate.

The relation of perceptions to reality is important in differentiating the perceptions of various groups, in judging their potential political consequences, and in considering means of bringing perceptions into closer (or more distant) alignment with reality. The correspondence of perceptions to reality, or their deviations from it, increase considerably in interest when we know the information sources to which the perceiver has been exposed and the correspondence of those sources to reality.

There are several difficulties in relating perceptions to reality. First of all, perceptions, as noted earlier, are often so vague and complex that whether or not they correspond to reality is not easily assessed. Second, some aspects of perceptions (such as the affect that accompanies them) cannot be related to reality in the sense of being measured against it. Third, and more important, perceptions of the military balance are not always in the form of simple factual statements. That the Soviet Union has so many more missiles than the United States may be easily assessed against reality. However, many of the perceptions of military reality, as one meets them in articles, editorials, and other sources, do not correspond with any readily defined "reality." Perceptions of the balance, for instance, may take the form of predictions that the United States or Soviet Union could win an intercontinental strategic war, make a successful first strike, or do a variety of other things more effectively than the other side if conditions so necessitated. Obviously, such statements cannot now be verified against "reality." Even statements that have a past or present time-reference can also provide the same difficulties. For example, statements that refer to the past or present military worth of French nuclear capabilities are not statements on whose "reality status" there will be ready agreement.

When no clear understanding of "reality" exists in a given situation, the observation and discussion of people's perceptions are likely to be distorted because the investigator's own vague "reality" differs from the vague "reality" of his subjects and influences his perceptions of the subject's perceptions. Thus, a psychiatrist who thought we were close to a nuclear war during the Cuban missile crisis viewed a calm attitude toward the crisis by his subjects as representing a psychiatrically alarming perception of the situation.

There are, of course, a substantial number of relatively clearcut aspects of the military reality, and the problems just indicated do not prevent us from analyzing how well perceptions of the military balance correspond with these more measurable aspects.

DIFFERING MILITARY BALANCES AS OBJECTS OF PERCEPTIONS

In inquiring into perceptions of the strategic balance, the NATO balance, the naval balance, or the global, overall balance, we must recognize that these divisions and their definitions are those of the investigator and do not necessarily preexist in the minds of our subjects. Presumably, we can induce our subjects, if we interview them, to consider the balance separately in various military sectors and in the terms that we specify, but we should remember that these may be our constructions, not theirs. This consideration is also pertinent in describing perceptions reported in the various media. We may be able to sort out statements made in an editorial, in a political speech, or in an article into several sectors (strategic, naval, etc.), but these divisions may not have had much independent existence in the mind of the writer. This, of course, does not mean that it is unjustified to do the sorting out. It only means that the conclusions we draw may be different according to whether it is we or the writer who do the sorting. Thus, the statements of some subjects may reflect only a view concerning a vague, overall balance and may not be accompanied by any sense of, or conviction about, individual sector balances, even though some statements may permit classification by the investigator into various military sectors.

The investigator's own definition of the military balance may also vary in different research contexts. Thus, sector divisions and definitions appropriate for studying some types of subjects (mass leaders, naive/sophisticated, and so forth) may not be appropriate for others. Or the definition of the balance during a crisis may differ from one used in a steady-state period in order to emphasize certain components that have special relevance in particular confrontations.

The Strategic Balance

From the investigator's standpoint, "strategic balance" refers to capabilities for nuclear intercontinental war. "Capabilities" may be characterized by number of bombs, warheads, and carriers, by accuracy and reliability, by active defenses, civil defense, and vulnerability to first attack, by command and control, warning, and reconnaissance capabilities.

Evidently, even a very summary account of these aspects of Soviet or U. S. capabilities together with even the most simplified account of their dynamic interactions would take several rather substantial paragraphs or pages. The attempt to establish equivalences between them might require a good deal of further elaboration. Any serious attempt to reduce these multiform capabilities to a few abbreviated strategic "capability coefficients" would require a forbiddingly complex set of intellectual operations and justifications. Such comparisons might require imputing the same purpose to the strategic capabilities of the United States and the Soviet Union, an imputation which our subjects may or may not make. The investigator might not reduce the components of the strategic balance to a simple expression, but this does not mean that it is necessarily a difficult task for his subjects. Their lesser sophistication, more limited information, or simply lesser preoccupation may make it possible for them to reduce a complex reality to a simple expression. Even specialists in military affairs might not integrate all relevant components of the balance into their perception. This does not exclude them from having a rough weighting system and a "coefficient" of strategic capability.

Two different accounts by subjects should be distinguished: (1) statements which the subject provides without constant prodding by the investigator, that is, what the subject provides more or less spontaneously; and (2) statements elicited only under more detailed questioning. Whether the latter are to be viewed as part of the subject's perception will depend on the uses to which their accounts are going to be put.

It is likely that, for many persons, military capabilities in the sense of materiel are less understandable, less interesting, or less relevant than notions concerning what each nation can do to the other.

A view that the Soviet Union has more Intercontinental Ballistic Missiles than the United States may be ignored, and if not ignored it may, nonetheless, be associated with the view that the Soviet Union would not dare to engage in a first strike or risk other types of military undertakings. Particular beliefs concerning deterrence (or nondeterrence) may be associated with a wide range of capabilities imputed to the United States and the Soviet Union.

In addition to beliefs concerning what each country might be able to undertake are beliefs concerning the outcomes of such undertakings. Who would "win the war," or who would suffer least damage, if there were an intercontinental war may be the principal modes in which some subjects perceive the strategic balance. It may be possible to trace such beliefs to prior beliefs about weapon systems, but beliefs about "who would win" may shape beliefs about the materiel balance and not the other way around. Ideas concerning what each nation can or cannot do, in both military and political uses, with their capabilities may represent the real characterization of military strength that individuals carry around in their heads.

These considerations could lead us to include national will in perceptions of the military balance. Similarly, technological ingenuity and economic resources may be viewed as important components of military power, particularly when relative military power is viewed as a developing and changing status. The perceived direction of this change may affect the perception of the current strategic balance.

The NATO Central Front Balance

Compared with the strategic sector, the NATO Central Front balance probably involves a more complex set of capabilities, especially because of manpower and mobilization factors; political and alliance relations; troop and population morale; the longer time period over which, in the event of war, military capabilities would probably be exercised; and the numerous interactions over this longer period of time of all the complex strategic and tactical elements that compose warfare involving large numbers of troops with all their supporting arms and services. Room for the intervention of the unpredictable seems particularly great in NATO scenarios.

All these factors affect not only the definition of the Central Front balance but render extraordinarily difficult the task of arriving at a statement of the "real" or "true" balance with which perceptions are to be compared. This difficulty already existed in the strategic sector but is almost certainly magnified in the NATO case. Thus, for example, the "real" balance certainly is affected, on the NATO side, by the reliability with which alliance forces would, in the event of war, perform their roles, and, on the Soviet side, by whether the non-Soviet Warsaw Pact forces fight loyally with the Soviets, do not fight at all, or actively sabotage Soviet military action. Not only will the "real" balance be different according to the probability of these events, but the perceived balance will similarly vary as one or another perceiver attaches more or less importance or plausibility to one factor or another.

The tendency to use numerical indices (number of divisions, number of aircraft, number of tanks, etc.) may occur here just as it can and does occur in many perceptions of the strategic balance. But in the NATO case perceivers are more likely to give weight to factors such as morale and political forces. These may produce a perception of the balance that deviates markedly from a perception based largely on materiel and manpower, that is, on material forces.

Strategic balance is likely to be viewed by most perceivers in terms of its significance for an intercontinental nuclear war having relatively few major variants. The NATO balance may, on the contrary, be viewed through a greater range of possibilities—from a full tactical nuclear war on all NATO fronts down to a "border straightening" operation. In any event, perceptions of the NATO balance probably should be described relative to various strategic objectives of the two sides, and this will require investigating these objectives as they exist in the perceiver's mind (if their spontaneous statements are being examined) or perhaps imposing a specific definition of these objectives on the perceivers (if they are being interviewed).

It is possible, of course, to assess U.S. and Soviet forces in terms of some abstract definition of strength that ignores any particular use or application of them. The balance is then viewed as a function of certain characteristics such as number, speed, accuracy, weight, reliability, whose goodness is a linear function of the size of the numbers and bears no specified relation to any objective or situation. This abstract, rather than war-fighting, characterization of the forces is less likely to dominate perceptions of the NATO balance than it would perceptions of the strategic balance.

The Naval Balance

The naval balance is not easily separable from the strategic balance since the latter includes the sea-launched missile forces and capabilities for operating against them. Like the strategic and NATO balances, the naval balance may present itself to subjects not as a certain set of forces but rather in terms of who is capable of doing what to whom. The perceived relation between physical and functional capabilities may be far from simple.

People may conceive of strategic intercontinental conflicts and NATO wars as independent forms of conflict, but are not so likely to think of naval warfare as occurring independently of either a NATO conflict or an overall strategic war. Limited naval warfare in some portion of the globe certainly is not to be excluded but it is an empirical question whether many people think of the naval balance in this way. On the other hand, naval forces are readily viewed as assisting in local interventions in various parts of the world. The strength of U. S. and Soviet strategic and European forces are most readily viewed in terms of the outcome of a conflict between them, but the "goodness" or strength of U. S. and Soviet naval forces can easily be viewed in many circumstances in terms of each nation's relative ability to perform vis-à-vis a third party rather than against each other. In this sense, U. S. and Soviet naval forces may be compared in the same way as one compares U. S. and Soviet airlift capabilities in contexts not implying an open conflict between the two countries.

The Global Balance

The military specialists may be most at home in speaking of a military balance in various sectors such as the strategic sector, the European (NATO) theater, or the naval sector. Other perceivers of the military scene may, however, have images or beliefs concerning some overall global military balance. This seems to be involved in various expressions concerning shifts in "global power"— who can force the world to do its bidding, or who is riding the wave of the future. The "global balance," to the extent that it corresponds to a real image or idea in people's minds, is probably more of a compound of military, political, and economic power than is true of the three individual sector balances considered so far. It probably has a heavy strategic component. Perceptions of "global power," where they exist, may be the product of perceptions of sector balances, but the inverse causality is not at all implausible.

PERCEIVERS

The principal classes of subjects, that is, perceivers, in which we may be interested are:

Political leaders. How narrowly or broadly we define this group will depend on the political structure of the country with which we are dealing. We will generally want to include here the principal advisers, official and unofficial, of the political leaders. One must recognize that their public statements on the military balance will not necessarily represent their views.

Bureaucracy. Certain sectors of officialdom, especially in such areas as national defense and foreign affairs, are clearly of interest, both because of their independent influence and their advice and information-giving functions to policy and decision-making levels.

Military. The military of a country is of interest for several reasons—as advisers to the government and as planners and decision makers whose decisions and policies may be influenced by their perceptions of the balance.

Parliamentarians. Parliamentarians are important because of their policy and legislative responsibilities and their influence on budgetary matters. Their accessibility through parliamentary debates and political speeches and their possible predictive value for the perceptions of the less accessible political leaders give them considerable importance.

The "literati." Here I include journalists, academicians, publicists, professional national security writers and analysts, and the like. This is probably an important group in influencing almost all other groups whose opinions are of interest. The effect of literati perceptions can hardly be understood by simply examining their opinions and the degree of agreement and disagreement among them. The influence of the literati requires fairly intensive investigation of the ways in which literati discussions, pronouncements, and debates affect each other and finally enter into other forms of literature and into the minds of the political classes, various special elites, and the public. Because of their actual or potential influence, the sources of the perceptions of the literati is a subject of capital importance. The role of political figures and government officials in influencing literati perceptions of the balance is of particular importance and probably varies substantially in different societies.

The Public. This residual term embraces anyone not included above, but more particularly it refers to the perceptions made available through public opinion polls, questionnaires, and academic studies of various major population sectors.

The value of studying more accessible groups may be substantial even though their perceptions of the military balance may be of less interest. One aim of perception studies is to understand the effect of particular types of events and information on perceptions. It is likely that dramatic events and announcements produce similar reactions in a wide variety of groups. The intrusion of nonrational factors in perceptions may very likely tend to uniformize the responses of different groups. Given the cost and difficulty of gaining access to some groups, studies of reactions to certain classes of events in groups of lesser interest could still be worthwhile. Naturally, the value of one group as a predictor of the reactions of another group would be greatly increased if we could compare the reactions of the two groups in two or three instances.

The Soviets do not seem to share our almost exclusive concern with high-level perceptions. They have considered it useful to influence the perceptions of their own and foreign publics on military affairs.

What countries are most relevant to study?

The answer to this question will depend on which objectives of perception studies are of primary interest. The perceptions of major allies and of potential antagonists are clearly of interest. But the policies of major allies are not independent of what lesser allies do. Thus, the perceptions of the military balance in a small country may have repercussions in larger countries. In addition, the position taken by a "minor" country in crisis situations may have crucial positive or negative consequences over a very wide political and military arena.

Similar considerations may apply to neutrals. The "one-world" character of today's international affairs makes it hazardous to ignore "unimportant" countries. Some countries may deserve attention, not because of their political significance, but because responses to certain types of events may be easier to study there. The ability to extrapolate results is, of course, important in these cases.

Substantial attention should be given to the perceptions of various sectors of the United States itself. It is almost certain that the perceptions of important sectors in the United States are a primary source for the perceptions of other countries. Besides, we are likely to understand better how perceptions in other countries arise if we are able to understand how the perceptions of U.S. elites and publics develop.

SOURCES OF PERCEPTIONS

With this section, we enter into topics that are predominantly empirical and require the clarification that only data can give. Nonetheless, a few relevant comments can be made.

A knowledge of the sources from which people draw their perceptions of the U.S.-USSR balance would serve two principal purposes: (1) It might enable us to infer the perceptions that people hold of the balance. Obviously this may be a risky type of inference because exposure to a source does not necessarily mean attention to what the source provides. Nor can we assume that people either believe or agree with the information or attitudes expressed by the sources. And, not everyone using the same information will come to the same conclusion. However, for some population sectors of special interest, such as the political leadership, we may be able to specify sources in which confidence is high and thus be able to make less risky inferences concerning the perceptions of the group. Besides, the mere preference by a perceiver for certain sources may in itself provide us with a good guess as to his views. (2) A knowledge of the sources from which people draw their information is indispensable for understanding how perceptions are formed and changed.

We often think of the sources of perception as information on the military balance that is conveyed either by the written or spoken word. However, perceptions of the balance can also be shaped by the political and military actions of countries. Anything from shoe-banging in the United Nations to the invasion of Czechoslovakia (1968) may influence perceptions of the U.S.-USSR balance. Actions as a source of perceptions point up the fact that the same input may provide different people with rather different conceptions. Aggressiveness may be viewed by some as an indication of superiority and by others as an expression of frustration and a sense of inferiority.

The effect of inputs on perception may be highly variable whenever information about the U.S.-USSR balance is of an indirect character and leads to judgments of the military balance only by a process of inference. Thus we can distinguish media information on military capabilities from the media's influence through its presentations on political-military-economic events that influence judgments of the balance.

When information sources and perceptions of the balance coincide, we should not assume without further investigation that the information sources have produced this identity. The information sources may have been chosen largely because their statements agree with the judgments and attitudes of the subjects involved.

An important objective in studying sources of perceptions of the military balance is to understand not only the influence of sources on subjects but the influence of one source on another. We need some knowledge of how information and beliefs percolate from one source to another and finally become available to this or that sector of the population. If we content ourselves only with the knowledge of the source that immediately provided the information to a subject, we have only a limited idea of what the information process is. We need to trace how the source in question got its own information and established its own perceptions. Relations among the media, between official and unofficial sources, public and private sources, foreign and native sources will presumably all be involved.

Research on sources of information should seek to establish their credibility for different audiences. Some subjects acquire their perceptions by assimilating various bits of information on the balance which are integrated into a particular mental image of the military balance. Other subjects do not seek such information or, even if they are exposed to it, do not assimilate it. What they assimilate are judgments enunciated by persons who are deemed reliable. Their perceptions of the military balance are essentially perceptions of the views of their "opinion leaders."

The political class often has to communicate its views on a subject to the country. They may have both a private perception of the balance and a public one. One should not discount the incentives they have to make private views of the balance accord with publicly expedient views.

PERCEPTIONS AND REALITY

The distribution of perceptions by their reality-status, that is, by their coincidence with or deviation from reality, is another empirical topic. Here we only provide a few comments elaborating on those made earlier. The reality with which we wish to compare a perception is in fact another perception, ours, in which we have high confidence. On the other hand, the perceptions of our subjects may vary considerably with respect to the degree of confidence that the perceiver has in them. Thus we may find that certain perceptions accord with reality but the perceptions are held with a very low degree of confidence; this needs to be taken into account when we affirm the coincidence of reality (our perceptions) and the perceptions of others.

Difficulties in relating perceptions to reality may stem from decreased certainty about the reality, increased complexity of the perception, decreased clarity in the perceptions, or the noncommensurability of perception and reality. If research is based on interviews, some matters concerning the perceptions can be made subject to clarification, although we may find that in asking for clarification we are leading subjects to express opinions on matters about which they have not previously thought or about which they have no conviction. Clarification may not be possible in the case of materials taken from printed sources.

If both reality and perceptions are expressed by a complex of statements, representation of deviations from reality is difficult. Often, there is no way of establishing what elements have been put into a complex assessment and what weights have been attributed to them. Deviations of such perceptions from the reality assessment may represent differences with respect to what is viewed as relevant rather than disagreement on the facts.

There are two different aspects to a statement concerning the deviation of perceptions from reality. Let us suppose that the advantages or disadvantages in some aspect of the balance are expressed by ratios. A reality judgment may, for example, give the United States a 3:2 advantage. Perceiver X may express his perception as a 3:2 advantage for the Soviet Union, and perceiver Y may attribute an 8:1 advantage to the United States. On arithmetical grounds, perceiver Y is further from reality than perceiver X. On the other hand, Y is closer to reality insofar as he views the advantage as lying with the United States, whereas perceiver X views it as lying with the Soviet Union. There is no contradiction involved here, but the example points to the need to distinguish deviations in amount and in direction.

One must suppose that if we study perceptions over a considerable range of perceivers, time periods, and military sectors, we will generally find that the deviations of perceptions from reality vary considerably in both amount and direction. There may be some aspects of the military balance that at particular periods are very highly classified, and most perceptions may deviate substantially from reality, except in incidental cases where accordance with reality results more from an untutored guess than from any real knowledge or understanding. Assuming, however, that in most cases the deviations of perceptions from reality are distributed over a considerable range of values, we will want to account for these variations. Some rather obvious questions suggest themselves. Are the deviations associated with the class of perceivers? Thus, do the perceptions of the literati accord more with reality than, say, those of political leaders or parliamentarians or the public? Do perceptions of the balance accord better with reality in strategic warfare than in the NATO area? Have perceptions of the military balance shown a greater tendency to accord with reality as time has gone on and information has increased? Do dramatic individual events (e. g. , Czechoslovakia, 1968) produce sharp changes in the deviations?

Charles Wolf, Jr. has pointed out that, at a given moment, perceptions may deviate from reality but correspond with reality if the deviation is measured consistently with either a lead or a lag. It seems reasonable to suppose that for relatively well-informed subjects interested in military affairs the lead hypothesis is likely to apply, whereas for ill-informed persons and those relatively uninterested in military affairs the lag hypothesis is more relevant. For an informed and interested person, the prospective picture is probably just as interesting or even more interesting than current or past situations. He may thus assimilate information concerning rates of change which may lead him to develop a perception of the present situation which anticipates the future. The uninterested person is more likely to ignore the future and the present, and it may take some time for changes to make an impression on him, thus producing a lag. One difficulty with the foregoing is that if in fact an individual is very interested in, and very well-informed about, military affairs and the military balance, one might suppose that he would be able to avoid the tendency to predate the future that produces a lead deviation. The hypothesis seems more applicable to those who are moderately interested and informed.

Perceptions may show an inverse relationship to reality over a substantial period. This might occur in a situation in which a country with low capabilities makes strenuous efforts to persuade the world to the contrary and succeeds in so doing. This seems to be what, in fact, the Soviet Union did during the postwar period up to 1961-62. The Soviet Union, very sensitive to any imputation of weakness, expended a great deal of effort to convince the world that it was making enormous progress in nuclear weapons, manned bombers, and missiles. These attempts to conceal military weakness did lead substantial parts of the world to view the military balance over a number of years as quite the reverse of what it was.

A thorough account of the perceptions of the military balance would try to explain certain aspects of perceptions already reviewed, for example, the degree of confidence in one's judgment; the stability of perception; the affect attached to perception; the complexity or simplicity of perceptions (which is not the same as deviation from, or accordance with, reality); the tendency to view the balance in terms of rates of change rather than comparisons of the current status; variations in preferred information sources on the balance; interactions among sources; tendencies for perceptions to lag or lead; the variability of perceptions with respect to clarity and fuzziness; and variations in the elements incorporated in perceptions.

In preceding sections, we have necessarily touched on various mechanisms which bear on the explanation of perceptions of the military balance. These include the amount and nature of information available, the class of perceivers involved, the sources available, the tendency for perceptions to be formulated in terms of materiel or in terms of warfighting capabilities, the effect of crises on perception, the impact of first-hand visual perception of military materiel and operations.

THE IMPACT OF PERCEPTIONS

It is generally assumed, and quite correctly, that the military forces available to nations have played an enormous role in shaping

political as well as military history. It is evident that, until such
time as they are actually brought into play, the effect of these forces
on the behavior of nations is completely dependent on the perceptions
of them. When they are brought into play, the consequences of the
real, as distinguished from the perceived, balance of forces show
themselves. But even during war itself, the perception of the forces
as distinct from the forces themselves continues to play an important
role.

The impact of perceptions of the military balance might be
better understood if we examined how such perceptions influenced
political and military behavior in the past. In earlier ages, the fate
of a king or a great noble not infrequently rested on the outcome of
a single battle. Wars were often periods of mobilization and trans-
portation of troops, leading to a single big confrontation with the
enemy in a decisive battle, often with disastrous consequences for
one side. Since the outcome of a single battle was a chancy matter,
subject to many unpredictable occurrences, the outcome of war itself
became almost equally chancy. Political advisers especially and
some rulers from ancient China through to the sixteenth century in
the West continually stressed the dangers of wars in which one's fate
depended on the outcome of a single, unpredictable battle. To avoid
serious full-scale battles that in one day could lose him a kingdom,
Louis XI developed forces whose perception by his enemies, rather
than whose action in battle, would gain him his objectives. Awe-
inspiring fortifications, troops in a ready status, and forces of
substantial size were intended not so much to win battles as to make
them unnecessary. Such situations have an interesting resemblance
to the position of the major nuclear powers. By becoming, relatively
speaking, a war with one big battle, strategic nuclear war reduces
war again to the point where one's fate rests on the uncertainties of
a single event. A nuclear power might believe that a one-battle
nuclear war is more calculable and less chancy than the one-battle
wars of the past; but, given the stakes in a strategic nuclear conflict,
it would not take much caution to realize that this increased
calculability, if it exists, is offset by the greatly increased losses
if the calculations go wrong. In short, then, the aggressive nuclear
power of today is perhaps in the position of Louis XI who feared to
risk all on one battle but nonetheless used his military forces to
gain his ends. Perceptions, together with sparing military use,
substituted for full-scale military action.

In democracies, the perceptions of the public have considerable
importance because they affect both the freedom of leaders to expend
funds for military purposes and their freedom to utilize existing
forces for various political or military purposes. The morale of
forces themselves is not unrelated to how they perceive their relation

of strength to those whom they may, or are going to, meet in battle. The Soviets have consistently acted as if they believed that the perceptions of masses in the democracies concerning the military balance have a significant political effect. And it seems evident that indeed it does. Within the Soviet Union itself, the Party takes steps to ensure that the Soviet peoples have a firm conviction that their military forces are superior to those of any other nation. U. S. efforts in this direction used to rely largely on the efforts of certain patriotic societies and on Fourth of July oratory. Nowadays, the exigencies of funding, congressional debate, and the freer flow of information often mean that the images disseminated of U. S. military forces relative to other military forces are hardly those that orators would prefer. The varying consequences of overly optimistic and overly pessimistic perceptions need to be determined and distinguished.

Because of their influence on budgetary action and on political and military planning, the perceptions of political leaders and parliamentarians are obviously of great importance. There are several problems of first-rate importance here. Do parliamentarians provide greater support for a military force that they feel is inferior to that of a potential enemy, or are they more inclined to take supportive action if they feel that past expenditures in the military sector have given their nation forces superior to anyone who might challenge them? May not a conviction that past expenditures have led to military inferiority inspire defeatist budgetary and political action whereas a conviction of military superiority may stimulate further interest in maintaining this superiority (rather than a do-nothing attitude as is sometimes supposed)?

One aspect of perceptions of the military balance that is of particular interest is the fear of one's own strength. This seems to be a contemporary phenomenon. There has probably not been in the past a period in which a nation or some prominent sector of it has shown great anxiety because of its own military strength. Today, a significant strain of thought sees great nuclear or general military strength of one's own nation as leading to irresponsible or immoral behavior on the international scene. Thus, perceptions of actual or potential superiority in the United States have in some sectors led to demands for reducing this superiority. Perceptions of military inferiority may not, in these groups, stimulate apprehension but rather a sense of relief and satisfaction that the political and military freedom of national leaders has been constrained by this inferiority.

CONCLUSION

This study has sought to raise and systematize questions and problems relative to research in the area of military-balance perceptions. As stated in the introduction, it is no more than a general map of what, as yet, remains a vague and amorphous area of research. As work progresses in the field, it will be possible both to revise and refine the map. Considering the need of defense policy makers to have a better understanding of the perceptions element surrounding the development and use of military forces, it is hoped that refinements and revisions will not be too long in coming.

2

THE MISSING DIMENSION OF U.S. DEFENSE POLICY: FORCE, PERCEPTIONS, AND POWER

Edward N. Luttwak

THE PROBLEM

In comparing the overall strategic conduct of the United States with that of the Soviet Union, a sharp contrast emerges between the obvious Soviet emphasis on the psychological dimension of military policy and the equally obvious neglect of this dimension in the military policy of the United States.

The essentially psychological concept of deterrence has been prominent in U. S. defense planning for many years, and yet force-structure and weapon-system decisions are still made without explicit consideration of the impact of these decisions on others' perceptions of U. S. military power. For example, the entire structure of the Soviet armed forces reveals the intention to capitalize systematically on the widespread tendency to evaluate military power in simple numerical terms; U. S. force planners by contrast, tend to be guided by organizational preferences for high unit-quality and tend to discount numbers per se. In the strategic-nuclear sector, for example, it has been U. S. policy to remove weapons from the inventory as soon as they failed to meet the most exacting criteria of modernity. As against this, it has been Soviet policy to retain any weapon which could still be represented as serviceable. As a result, some 980 ICBMs and 322 B-52 bombers have been withdrawn from U. S. operational forces over the last decade and a half, while the Soviet Union has with a few exceptions retained in service virtually every strategic weapon it has ever deployed.

There were sound strategic, economic, and technical reasons for withdrawing weapons such as the Atlas ICBMs from the operational inventory. By the time the Strategic Arms Limitation negotiations were in progress, there were no Atlas ICBMs in the inventory to keep or withdraw. But the Minuteman 1 force was still intact. At a time when it was obvious that the force ceilings of a SAL accord would reflect primarily the numerical status quo, U. S. decision makers nevertheless chose to remove them to make way for the Minuteman 3s, instead of merely adding the new weapons to the old, as the Soviets were doing with SS-11s and SS-9s.

There was a critical inconsistency in U. S. policy which denied all importance to purely numerical factors in the context of force-structure decisions and then proceeded to give full diplomatic recognition to "mere numbers" in the context of international negotiations. The immediate effect of this policy was to set the stage for the advent of Soviet numerical superiority in ICBMs—a superiority formally recognized in the SAL-1 accords. The broader impact of the decision was manifest in the transformation of third-party perceptions of the strategic balance.

While there were a good many disparate factors at work in the Minuteman 1 decision, there can be little doubt that a major common denominator was the general tendency to ignore or at least discount the importance of perceptual factors. The notion that numbers, or any other "visible" indexes, had a certain definite value in themselves could hardly have influenced decision making since the perceptual dimension of deployment policy is refractory to quantitative evaluation—unlike the engineering or financial dimensions. Thus, it would indeed have to rest on vague and unsystematic propositions about what others may or may not think about U. S. strategic power. In a decision-making process that became increasingly mechanistic—particularly after 1961—in which greater and greater emphasis was placed on comparisons of variables that are easily quantifiable, wholly unquantifiable notions could hardly play a significant role. Even in the rare instances when they were admitted into the decision process, unsubstantiated contentions about the psychological (and therefore political) repercussions of force-structure or weapons-system decisions were thereafter discounted to the point of insignificance.

It is important to recognize the generality of this phenomenon. With a consistency that would be remarkable if it were accidental, Soviet force-structure decisions have tended to maximize the perceptible manifestations of Soviet military power, while an equally consistent neglect of perceptual factors is evident from the character of U. S. force structures. Far from being an isolated exception, the contrast between the unilateral withdrawal of the Minuteman 1 force and the retention of the Soviet SS-7s and SS-8s is reproduced in virtually every sector of military power, from the number of army divisions to the armament of surface combatants.

Under present plans, for example, the U. S. Army is to have a total of 16 active divisions, while at the last count the Soviet army had 68, more than ten times as many. The overall manpower ratio, by contrast, is of the order of 2. 15:1. It is known that only about one-third of the Soviet divisions are deployed continuously at full strength, so that a direct comparison would have to include U. S. reserve and National Guard forces also. Moreover, U. S. Army divisions are, of course, much larger than their Russian counterparts. If reorganized along Soviet lines—with smaller divisions and still smaller division-slices (i. e. , with diminished manpower in support and service forces outside divisions), and with the same proportion of understrength units—the U. S. Army could deploy roughly 78 "divisions" with its present manpower level, thus reducing very considerably the apparent numerical imbalance between the two armies.

While some have advocated such a Soviet-style organization for purely military reasons, there is no reason to believe, a priori, that the ground-force organization of the Soviet armed forces is in fact strategically and tactically superior to that of the U. S. In particular, it has not been demonstrated convincingly that the Soviet emphasis on ready combat power as opposed to sustained combat capability, or Soviet methods of whole-unit replacement and in-unit training, are preferable to U. S. priorities and methods. There is thus a prima facie case against the great strains and costs of such a reorganization—if strategic and tactical effectiveness are the only "outputs" to be maximized.

But if the comparison includes the perceptual-political dimension, it is no longer possible to reserve judgment on which of the two force structures is "better." It is abundantly clear that, ever since 1945, the Soviet Union has gained great political net benefits from the perceived superiority of its ground forces over those of the United States in Europe and those of NATO as a whole. And it is equally obvious that these images of a superior Soviet army have derived from and have reflected the superior number of Soviet divisions more than any other single index of ground-force capability. *

In countless official statements, reference has been made to the threat posed by the "160 Soviet divisions" or "200 Warsaw Pact divisions."[1] These were, of course, Western statements, in almost every instance aimed at domestic audiences in conjunction with the

---

*Virtually every press article touching on the issue includes a comparison of Warsaw Pact and NATO military strength case in terms of divisional counts; few articles proceed to mention other indexes (such as manpower totals or quality). Hardly any compare aggregate troop quantity and force quality.

annual budgetary struggle over defense expenditures. But the Soviets for their part have also used their information channels to amplify and project images of a war-winning Soviet army.

In the 1950s, these images of Soviet predominance on the ground served to counteract equally prevalent images of U. S. superiority in air power and technological superiority in general. In the 1960s, such images served to counteract perceptions on both sides of U. S. superiority in strategic-nuclear forces; images of a vastly superior Soviet ground force, capable of overrunning Western Europe, still persist.

There is no need to summarize here the post-1945 history of East-West relations in Europe in order to demonstrate that the Soviet Union has gained more than a mere psychological satisfaction from the widespread impression that its ground forces were vastly superior—by orders of magnitude—to those of the West. By translating what was at most a small measure of actual tactical superiority into the appearance of overwhelming strength, the Soviet Union has made tangible gains in the diplomatic arena, and it continues to do so.

In the absence of conflict, the political shadow cast by European perceptions of Soviet superiority on the ground sufficed to induce Western governments to make important concessions to the Soviet Union, accommodating Soviet demands that would otherwise have been rejected out of hand, or worse, ignored. The impact of this perceptual advantage has been manifest across the full range of East-West interactions in Europe, from the status-of-Berlin negotiations to the conduct of West European trade relations with the Soviet Union. It is, of course, difficult to disentangle the multiple factors involved in the conduct of trade relations. But neither is it essential for the argument to do so; the central fact that should never be lost sight of is that the Soviet Union remains much less important than, say, Italy. As a source of raw materials, it is quite outclassed in the energy sector by any one of several Persian Gulf oil exporters, and in the food and fiber sector, by the United States. As a source of investment capital and technological know-how for Europe, the Soviet Union ranks with Liechtenstein rather than, say, Austria. Hence the unique importance of military power as a constituent of overall national power for the Soviet Union. In contending with the purely military strength of the Soviet Union, the leaders of Western Europe have employed a mixture of deterrence and conciliation. In the latter lay the payoff as far as the Soviets were concerned.

It may be argued that in making concessions to the Soviet Union—the concessions which translated Soviet military strength into actual political leverage—the leaders of Western Europe were not being deluded by false images of Soviet superiority on the ground, but were motivated rather by realistic appreciations of the "true" balance of military power. According to this line of argument, the fact that the Soviets deployed their ground troops into many divisions, while U. S. and NATO forces were organized in fewer and larger divisions, was quite irrelevant. For policy-level appreciations of the balance of power were not based on misleading divisional counts but rather on "actual" Soviet capabilities, as well as on the imputed propensity of the Soviet Union to initiate a conflict.

Common sense would suggest that the national leaders of sophisticated Western European nations could hardly make an error so crude as to compare units that were quite unequal. But against this presumption there is a mountain of evidence which demonstrates beyond doubt that the terms of the comparison are almost always much closer to those suggested by simple divisional counts than, say, manpower counts. [2]

Comparisons of NATO and Warsaw Pact ground capabilities based on the single index of, for example, the actual troop strengths available to the two sides would be grossly inadequate, but at least they would be meaningful, if only partially so. By contrast, comparisons of divisional counts alone, strictly speaking, are quite meaningless, given the order-of-magnitude inequality between the units thus being counted. And yet Western perceptions of Soviet superiority on the ground do not correlate with the fractional advantages yielded by manpower comparisons but rather with much wider margins of advantage, which correspond quite closely to the meaningless comparisons of divisional counts. The consistency of this pattern of perceptions is much too great to make the correlation coincidental.

Further evidence of the saliency of purely numerical indexes is provided by another popular token of Soviet superiority: the greater number of Soviet battle tanks as compared to those of NATO in Europe. It is, of course, true that the Soviet inventory of battle tanks has always exceeded by far that of the NATO forces in Europe, or indeed of NATO members worldwide. But it is also true that, in comparing the strength of a defensive alliance with that of a force poised for the offensive, a straight comparison of the number of battle tanks on each side is a very poor guide to the relative capabilities on the defense and the offense respectively. It would be more useful, for example, to compare Warsaw Pact tank capabilities with NATO antitank capabilities (in which tanks do play an important role). As another approximation, it would also be less misleading to evaluate Soviet mobility forces as against NATO firepower, air support, and mine-warfare capabilities. But, in fact, such comparisons are hardly ever found in statements of "the military balance" in Europe. Instead, great prominence is given to the "40,000 tanks of the Soviet army," or to the "20,000 tanks" of the Warsaw Pact in Central Europe, as opposed to the "7,000 tanks" of NATO in the central sector. [3]

Quite apart from the tactical-operational considerations which invalidate the comparison, and aside from the inherent inadequacy of any comparison which excludes the "software" of morale, leadership, and planning in counting the hardware, there is also the fact that Soviet tanks have lost their former qualitative superiority, and are now on average considerably inferior to their British, West German, and U.S. counterparts. In spite of all these reasons for rejecting out of hand the simple tank-count as an index of military power, numerical tank comparisons are still featured as key indexes of ground-force capabilities.

Much the same state of affairs prevails in the naval sector of the superpower competition. From small beginnings, and in particular from a grossly inferior qualitative base, the Soviet navy has grown in quantity and apparent quality to the point where it can no longer be dismissed as an antagonist to the U.S. Navy. Indeed, there have already been the first suggestions that the proper goal of U.S. naval policy now should be to attain some form of "parity" with the Soviet navy or, at any rate, to concede some semblance of parity in the framework of bilateral naval limitation accords.

Given the utter superiority of the U.S. Navy when the naval competition first began in the immediate aftermath of World War II, and given the heavy investment in naval power made by the United States since then, the success of Soviet naval planners has been spectacular—in some ways more striking than Soviet achievements in other sectors of the arms competition. Without questioning, for the moment, the capabilities of the Soviet navy under realistic politico-military assumptions, it must be recognized that in the eyes of the world the Soviet navy has achieved some sort of rough parity with the U.S. Navy.

Once again, the perceptual factors that have served to form the impression in people's minds that the two navies have become some-how equivalent in power are denoted by their simple character: straightforward ship counts, and equally simple visual imagery, pseudoqualitative in character (Soviet warships are commonly described as "bristling with weapons"). It is ironic that the numerical parity between the two fleets was not brought about so much by the Soviets themselves as it was by the deliberate policy of U.S. naval planners. Between 1969 and 1975, the number of U.S. Navy vessels was reduced from 976 to 483 through the accelerated retirement of older and less capable warships. This drastic cut in the size of the fleet may or may not have been justified (the postdecision increases in operating costs certainly strengthens the argument in its favor), but right or wrong, the decision implied a very strong preference for unit

quality, as opposed to mere numbers, and a strong preference for
a fleet of fully operational warships over a much larger fleet kept
at a lower level of readiness. These preferences presumably
reflected strategic calculations about the respective worth of quality
versus quantity—and not merely bureaucratic tastes and traditional
preferences.

It is therefore noteworthy that at the very time when the decision
to opt for quality was being implemented, official navy spokesmen and
prominent retired officers began to popularize comparisons of the
U. S. and Soviet fleets cast in terms of the total number of warships
deployed, and even in terms of "ship-days" in particular areas of
deployment. [4] (Considerable currency was, for example, given to
assessments of the naval balance in the Eastern Mediterranean on
the occasion of the October 1973 crisis which were stated exclusively
in numerical terms.) Thus, the very people who decided to reduce the
numerical strength of the navy in order to upgrade present and future
quality immediately proceeded to neglect qualitative factors altogether
in popularizing straight numerical comparisons between the Soviet and
U. S. navies. *

It is, or should be, perfectly clear that the U. S. and Soviet
navies cannot be usefully compared by simple ship-counts or, for
that matter, in terms of gross tonnage—in which the U. S. Navy
remains superior by far. Given the profound structural differences
between the two navies, not even detailed and sophisticated materiel
comparisons are of any use. For example, the U. S. Navy has a
variety of offensive air capabilities as well as an opposed-landing
capability of major proportions, while Soviet capabilities in these
respects are still embryonic.

Nor can comparisons between the two fleets be made on the
basis of the presumed outcome of naval battles. For one thing, the
outcome of combat scenarios is predetermined by their tactical and
strategic assumptions to a degree unique to naval warfare. More
importantly, the utility of the two fleets is determined not only by
what they could do to each other in the event of all-out warfare between
the Soviet Union and the United States, but also by what they could do
to others, in less improbable circumstances. For example, in the
context of a "normal" Middle East crisis, the ability of the Soviet fleet
to destroy the Sixth Fleet in an all-out "splendid" missile strike is
simply irrelevant; in realistic political terms, what matters is that
the Sixth Fleet could land troops and provide air support (or air

---

*As a bureaucratic tactic, the quality-quantity switch may of
course make ample sense. In terms of world-wide perceptions of
U. S. naval power, it has been a disaster.

defense) for U. S. clients in the area, while the Soviet navy would
have the sole option of launching an all-out attack against the Sixth
Fleet or else doing nothing of substance (unless the shipping of local
powers is a worthwhile target for attack or defense).

All such considerations are now obscured by the prevalence of
simplistic numerical comparisons. Reiterated endlessly in official
statements before Congress and in speeches widely diffused by the
media, these ship-counts have created images which have become
international political realities, with manifest consequences on the
attitudes of political leaders the world over. While from the Soviet
Union there issues a steady stream of glorification of the Soviet navy,
the message relayed by U. S. media stresses the inadequacies of the
U. S. Navy and the loss of its former superiority; almost always, the
prime emphasis is on the ship-counts. Whatever the pressures of the
Congressional appropriations process, the public relations stance
of the navy should come under close scrutiny, for these comparisons
of U. S. and Soviet naval power, though aimed at domestic opinion, in
fact shape third-party perceptions of the naval segment of the overall
balance of military power. As such, these comparisons play a
significant part in determining the respective standing of the two
superpowers, and, therefore, their influence on the world scene.

PERCEPTIONS AND THE POLITICAL UTILITY OF ARMED FORCES

The political utility and military effectiveness of a given
structure of armed forces exist in different worlds: one, the world
of appearances, impressions, and the culturally determined value
judgments of international politics; the other, the world of physical
reality in actual warfare. This fundamental difference, that is, the
difference between force and power, has only been clearly analyzed
quite recently in the literature of political science. Without delving
into the complexities of the distinction, some of the more salient
differences may be noted: Force is definitive, its operation being
physical, unambiguous and direct; power, on the other hand, is
indirect since it is a function of what others are willing to do in
response to the tacit or explicit demands of the powerful. Power
must be recognized by others if it is to function, whereas force
functions in and of itself. Hence the centrality of perceptions in the
workings of power and their crucial role in determining the political
utility of armed forces.

If "true" combat capabilities were always perceived correctly,
then all distinctions between power and force, or between political
utility and military effectiveness, would not matter at all from the
viewpoint of defense planning. If there were perfect information, and

if the assumptions under which forces are evaluated by all parties
were identical, actual and perceived capabilities would always have to
be identical also. But in reality there are many factors which tend
to make for a significant and sometimes gross divergence between the
two.

First and most obvious is the simple problem of information.
Only a handful of the 142 governments now represented in the United
Nations have independent means of intelligence collection with which
to establish what weapons and what forces are deployed by the United
States, the Soviet Union, and any other power not immediately
adjacent to them.

Second, there is the problem of evaluation. Even with perfect
data on all the tangible aspects of military power, it remains impossible to arrive at uniform assessments of power balances—which
convert material and human inputs into true potential combat
capabilities—by taking due account of the intangibles of training,
managerial efficiency, morale, and leadership. Hardware comparisons
are not merely inadequate on their own, but worse than useless. They
do not so much convey only a part of reality as obscure reality
altogether. On the other hand, as soon as evaluations go beyond the
tangibles, they must include subjective assessments of genuine
imponderables, such as leadership and morale. When this is done—
and it must be done—evaluations will cease to be uniform even if all
evaluators have access to identical data on the tangible components
of military power.

Third, there is the problem of salience. The relevance of
different types of combat capability differs sharply according to the
roster of antagonists. The extensive antisubmarine capabilities of
the U. S. Navy may be an important segment of the deterrent spectrum
vis-à-vis the Soviet Union with its large submarine force. But the
same antisubmarine capabilities would not count for much in deterring
Syria, which has no real submarine force at all. Even where the
contrast is less extreme, it will readily be appreciated that the
salience of a given array of capabilities differs from context to
context, and, specifically, that the physical reality of U. S. military
capabilities breaks down into many separate perceived realities vis-
à-vis as many separate antagonists.

For these reasons, the images of military capabilities perceived
by others may differ greatly as between different perceivers. In
general, perceptions will not be an accurate reflection of the
"objective" reality of physical capabilities as revealed from time to
time by the test of actual warfare. It follows that the optimization
of combat capabilities will not simultaneously insure the optimization
of the "power" projected by any given force-structure. Hence, if the
overall politico-military "output" of the nation's investment in its

military establishment is to be maximized, explicit consideration must be given to the perceptual factor. Indeed, the latter must be elevated into a major criterion of force planning and deployment decision making. In other words, in order to extract maximum benefits from U. S. military forces, their structure and modes of operation must be deliberately aimed at projecting images of power, in ways that are readily absorbed by the world-wide audience of political actors and opinion makers.

THE MODALITIES OF PERCEPTION

Although they are complex, the data which describe physical weapon capabilities will at least be unidimensional: if the range of a missile is stated at 5,000 miles, this will be so whether the audience for the statement is the high command of the RAF or an Indian peasant. By contrast, for the reasons listed above, broader perceptions of military power will differ as between different classes of perceivers.

We can distinguish between at least three classes: (A) policy-makers and inner elite members with access to privileged information (and technical advice), and with a strong professional interest in politico-military issues; (B) media operatives and other opinion-makers with access to large information flows, not necessarily detailed, and with a less concentrated interest in politico-military issues; and (C) the general public, with access only to the data conveyed by mass media, and whose level of attention to politico-military issues varies from the very intense (e. g. , in countries at war) to the very low, the latter being more common.

A second distinction can be made a priori as between different types of national systems. For practical purposes, four categories of countries may be usefully distinguished:

Type I: economically developed modern societies, with democratic forms of government. In these, the perceptions of all three classes have an impact on the total policy process. This group includes the United States, most NATO members, Australia, Israel, and a few other countries.

Type II: highly centralized totalitarian societies. In these, only the perceptions of Class A (policy makers and inner elite) will have an impact on policy formation over the short and medium terms. This category includes the USSR and the People's Republic of China (PRC), Cuba, Vietnam, and North Korea.

Type III: underdeveloped, modernizing larger states whose governance is authoritarian but not totalitarian. In these, the perceptions of classes A and B (opinion makers) both count, but not

the perceptions of Class C (mass publics). This category includes
Brazil, Egypt, India, and Iran.

Type IV: under developed small states with ruling micro-
elites which have no access to worthwhile privileged information.
In these, Class A and Class B perceivers cannot be usefully
separated: both rely on imported mass-media information which is
usually of Western origin. This category includes most of the 142
members of the U. N.

From the above categorization, it can be deduced directly that
the following classes of perceivers are of practical significance:

Type I	Type II	Type III	Type IV
A	A	A	None
B	—	B	—
C	—	—	—

The omission of Class C perceivers in Type III countries follows by
definition: even if their opinions counted for something in the policy-
making process, there is no practical way of reaching this group.
Radio media may convey facts and figures to this audience, but in the
absence of the necessary context such facts and figures are bound to
be virtually meaningless. The omission of all classes under Type IV
is explained by the dependence of the one relevant group (the small
ruling elite) on out-of-country information sources, i. e. , the general
Western—or more rarely Soviet—media; while the former are
already covered under Type I, Soviet media are in any case beyond
reach. No matter what steps could be taken to enhance the visibility
and perceptual impact of U. S. power, controlled outlets such as
TASS would process the information unfavorably.

It is obvious that the perceptions of Class A observers in Type
I and Type II countries are of central importance: they collectively
determine those balances of perceived power that govern the external
conduct of the most important states on the world scene. Nevertheless,
it is by no means self-evident that these two groups ought to be the
principal targets of perceptual manipulation addressed specifically
at these groups as opposed to all other groups. This is because Class
A observers in Type I and Type II countries are likely to be
refractory to such perceptual manipulation: while a shift in the
perceptions of such groups would count for much more than a similar
shift in the perceptions of any other groups, it is also likely to be
very much more difficult to achieve. For one thing, it is to be
expected that data derived from U. S. actions would reach Class A
observers in both types of countries through the medium of sophisticated channels of information with a high technical content. Such

channels ought to be able to filter out factors that distort perceptions of military power, and the technical analysis of the incoming data will normally resist manipulation.

It remains to define, at least conceptually, what military-force characteristics are liable to be salient in the perception of non-technical observers. What follows is a brief review of the propositions that seem most plausible.

Time is discounted. The general tendency is to anticipate future changes in military capabilities. An obvious example is the public reaction to such events as the Soviet test of a fission device in 1949. The reaction was not that the Soviet Union would become more "powerful" in X years, when it would deploy operational forces equipped with fission bombs; it was rather that the Soviet Union had become more powerful, as of the time word of the fission test was released. Even though this foreshortening of time was erroneous (i. e. , it failed to take deployment lags into account), the impact was real nevertheless. The Soviet Union did indeed become more power-ful, in that its ability to deter or compel—a function of others' reactions to its presumed capabilities—increased as soon as the news of the fission test was released.

Time is also discounted in a more subtle sense: there is a general tendency to aggregate military capabilities, economic resources, and technical ingenuity into a common perception of power. While defense planners must contend with the fact that in a central conflict it will probably be impossible to convert economic resources into deployed military capabilities in a timely manner, it appears that even Class B perceivers in Type I countries continue to treat the mobilization potential of societies as part of their current strength on the world scene.

The most direct consequence of the discounting of time is that in determining perceptions of military capabilities, especially in comparative terms, the impact of perceived rates of change may equal or outweigh the impact of current capabilities. A statement such as "in 1985 the Soviet air force will become more 'powerful' than the USAF unless . . ." is not perceived primarily as meaning that the USAF is more "powerful" now; instead, it will tend to enhance perceptions of Soviet air power in the present. The common practice of U. S. spokesmen, official and otherwise, of stressing Soviet progress in this or that sector of the competition therefore has a particularly negative impact on third-party perceptions of the balance of power.

There are sharp differences in the perceptual impact of different kinds of information about military capabilities, at any rate as far as nontechnical observers are concerned. Initial guidance on the relative ease of absorption of different forms of information can be provided by the content of commercial advertising (correcting for cultural bias); this is particularly useful because of the objective feedback that guides its content (i. e. sales figures). By inference from the practices of commercial advertising, the following propositions may be derived.

Force-level figures are readily absorbed because numbers are conceptually simple in themselves, (as opposed to nontrivial qualitative information). However, if numerical descriptions of military forces are to have a strong perceptual impact, the units involved must be vividly meaningful to the audience. For example, "divisions," "tanks," and to a lesser extent, "ICBMs" are meaningful units, in the sense that nontechnical observers believe that they understand what these terms describe. This is so even if in fact the meaning of these units is being misunderstood—which is especially likely to be the case in comparisons of different national forces, where combat formations are often unequal in substance even if their nomenclature is identical.

Further, if numbers are to have an impact, context must be supplied, usually by means of comparisons. For example, the statement that the Soviet Union has 1,618 ICBMs may be interpreted to mean that the Soviet Union is weak, since a good many nontechnical observers seem to think that the superpowers have "thousands" of ICBMs. By contrast, the statement that the Soviet Union has 1,618 ICBMs versus 1,054 for the United States is readily understood in a broadly correct sense (i. e., the Soviet Union has "more").

While numbers are readily absorbed, they are not computed easily. Hence, the perceptual impact of multiple numerical statements is actually likely to be degraded, unless the implication of the numbers is cumulative, (e. g., "The Soviet Union has 600 more ICBMs and 200 more SLBMs . . . " versus "The Soviet Union has 600 more ICBMs but 250 fewer bombers, 200 more SLBMs but 300 fewer cruise missiles, etc.").

Performance data is not readily absorbed unless a clearly understood index of normality is provided. In describing the constituents of military power this will usually be a maximal benchmark, (e. g. the "world's fastest aircraft" versus "aircraft flown at Mach 3.8").

Qualitative information may be readily absorbed also if it can be conveyed in visual terms, or at least in vivid verbal imagery. Nontechnical observers can see an aircraft carrier, in life or photography. Past exposure to either will enable such observers to visualize aircraft carriers on the basis of nonvisual information. By contrast, nontechnical observers cannot visualize radar or sonar equipment. The same consideration applies to the generally higher-impact information on capabilities-in-use. Again, nontechnical observers can visualize the meaning of "three tank divisions advancing" but they cannot visualize the (possibly much more striking) performance of radar, sonar, or other such systems. Verbal imagery may be vivid and perceptually effective even when the operations described cannot be seen at all, as in the case of a successful ballistic-missile intercept ("Like hitting a fly in outer space"; "like hitting a bullet with a bullet").

Actual personal exposure to the reality of on-going military activities can have a wholly disproportionate impact on perceptions of military capabilities. An observer exposed to the sights and sounds of flight operations on board an aircraft carrier may thereafter discount all kinds of less vivid information that would counteract his own personal impressions of formidable power (e. g. , data on Soviet anticarrier capabilities).

Nontechnical observers tend to be overimpressed by technologically advanced qualitative features of military equipments, regardless of their actual contribution to force-effectiveness. Hence "nuclear aircraft carrier" has a greater impact on nontechnical perceptions than "aircraft carriers. " Similarly, the importance of bombers may be discounted because of a tendency to regard them as "old-fashioned," as compared to ballistic missiles. (Given enough exposure, the cruise missile may in turn displace the ballistic missile as the advanced strategic weapon par excellence.)

As some of the above indicates, perceptions find their place in frames of reference which are themselves the cumulative residue of earlier perceptions. The perceivers are "educated" progressively through exposure to successive layers of information. Most of the world's supply of data on military power emanates from the U. S. Department of Defense. The remainder largely originates from specialized publications with good access to U. S. defense officials and defense contractors. Soviet and other adversary primary sources provide only a small fraction of the military data and hardly any numerical data at all.

Similarly, information on military capabilities world-wide reaches the global audience—elite or otherwise—primarily through U. S. media channels, notably the weekly newsmagazines, the major newspapers, news-agency reports, and technical journals. Non-U. S. Western media convey a distinctly smaller amount of data on military capabilities. Non-Western media, including Soviet media, convey very little original data; in fact, even specialized Soviet military publications rely almost exclusively on data quoted from Western media in covering U. S. , Soviet, and Chinese military capabilities.

IMPLICATIONS FOR U. S. DEFENSE POLICY

The propositions set out above are no more than hypotheses; they need to be elaborated in much greater detail and then tested through opinion research, especially elite-opinion research. But it is not premature to consider the possible implications for U. S. defense policy. Three broad policy approaches to the problem present themselves.

The first would be to formulate and implement a purposeful information policy for the Department of Defense on the lines of institutional advertising. The idea would be to augment the political output from existing force structures and modes of deployment by enhancing the images of power they generate and by overcoming their perceptually negative features. Elements of such a policy would range, for example, from detailed and repeated explanations of the vast difference between Soviet and U. S. army divisions to the systematic exposure of elite observers to suitable U. S. capabilities in action (e. g. , many more visits to aircraft carriers, especially when engaged in flight operations), to the upward redesignation of combat formations. This cosmetic approach would require no actual changes in force structures and modes of deployment. The recent redesignation of U. S. Navy warships—whatever its motives—is an example of such a cosmetic policy in action; large destroyers have become cruisers, the patrol frigates have become guided-missile frigates, and so on.

The second approach would seek to change the reality rather than attempt to present an unchanged reality differently. An example of this more drastic approach—which may entail more military-organizational costs than political benefits—would be to restructure the ground formations of the U. S. Army to yield 32 smaller divisions instead of the planned 16, or even to produce 160 "combat groups" (battalions). Another kind of structural change would be to change the configuration of warships so as to augment their visible armament (presumably at the expense of invisible but more useful capabilities). A nonstructural change in the mode of operation of current forces would be to increase the exposure of attack submarines. (Their capabilities are usually overlooked in the semiofficial estimates of Soviet and U. S. naval capabilities in Mediterranean conflict scenarios which are now in circulation.) It is evident that, if taken to extremes, this approach would lead to the deployment of "cardboard" military forces, on the lines of the Italian army and navy of the interwar period which were used, in effect, as theatrical props to support an activist foreign policy.

But in a less extreme form this approach is not to be dismissed. There are, for example, a good many tactical analysts who already advocate the abandonment of the large-division army (and marine) force structure for purely military reasons, without regard to the perceptual impact of more, albeit smaller, units. Similarly, there are many naval analysts who question the wisdom of continued investment in small numbers of very large hulls in the presence of the single-shot, ship-killing missile. Again, such analysts argue the merits of more and smaller hulls independently of the possible impact on world-wide perceptions of U. S. naval power that a larger fleet might have. Much the same line of argument is followed in regard to tactical aircraft and battle tank design. (The investment cost of a 35-ton tank with simple fire-control and other ancillaries might be not much more than a third of the expected XM-1 cost.) With regard to each of these questions controversy continues. In circumstances where the merits of the case are evenly divided on cost and military-effectiveness grounds, introduction of the perceptual factor under this second approach might legitimately swing the balance.

Finally, there is a third approach to the problem, one which would avoid the extremes of the minimalist "cosmetic" approach, on the one hand, and of the maximalist approach of perceptual-optimization, on the other. This third approach would legitimize the perceptual dimension of defense policy, making it an accepted component of the overall problem of maximizing the political-military utility of the defense effort as a whole. Under this approach, estimates of the perceptual impact of the various alternatives under consideration would be taken into account in the decision-making process, along with the established variables of cost, technical performance, tactical effectiveness, strategic suitability, and so on.

In practice, this would entail the development of "perceptual-impact analyses" which would be injected on a routine basis into the decision process on weapon-system procurement, force planning, and peacetime force deployment. Detailed guidelines for the conduct of such "perceptual-impact analyses" cannot be developed in the abstract, but would require ad hoc formulation, consistent with the particular nature of the audience, of the salient forms of communication and the major features of the preexisting perceptual-political context. For example, a perceptual-impact analysis of a small augmentation (or reduction) of the U. S. ground forces in West Germany would entail a different "audience" than a perceptual-impact analysis of the B-1 bomber program, and it would also entail different forms of communication and a different preexisting context.

In the former case it might be determined, for example, that the primary audiences are West German and other NATO Class A and Class B groups, as well as the Chinese and Soviet Class A audiences, more or less in that order of priority. The primary forms of communication are liable to be indirect, with the German mass public receiving the data through German media, which are apt to transmit the information without the qualifications and mention of counter-vailing factors that the original official release is liable to include, and which U. S. media are more likely to include. Salient features of the preexisting perceptual-political context might include the high

profile of Soviet ground capabilities and the residual uncertainties
that still attend the U. S. commitment to European defense. In the
second case, however, the primary audience for the B-1 bomber
program is the Soviet Class A group; the forms of communication
will include internal Soviet intelligence channels, and the preexisting
perceptual-political context may include notions of manned-bomber
effectiveness—a residue of Backfire advocacy—while the notion that
bombers are generally "old-fashioned" is much more likely to be
prevalent among secondary audiences such as those of Western
Europe.

    Having determined the relevant audiences and forms of com-
munication, and having defined the salient features of the preexisting
perceptual-political context, the next step would be to formulate
tentative guidelines for the perceptual dimension of the decision. At
this stage, all sorts of questions would arise: Does the West German
public know how many U. S. troops are in their country? Or rather,
what proportion of the public has a generally accurate notion of the
number of troops? To what extent is the number of troops regarded
by Class A and B audiences as important per se in NATO deterrence?
How does this square with the seemingly still prevalent idea that
NATO strategy is primarily strategic-nuclear, with a tripwire ground
force component? Or is this idea no longer current? and so on. The
hypothetical guidelines themselves (generally based on the propositions
on perception modalities set out above), and such subordinate
questions, would next have to be defined precisely so that they can
be tested through actual opinion research, primarily elite-opinion
research. Finally, on the basis of tested theories, a reasoned and
documented perceptual input would be made into the decision process,
alongside with the cost-analysis, tactical-strategic and branch-
preference inputs. While never as exact as inputs based on actual
(not planned) costs and performance, the perceptual inputs thus
developed should not entail conspicuously greater uncertainties than
many of the established criteria that now govern defense decision
making. Politics and perceptual analysis are not exact sciences,
but then neither is the study of war.

    Especially in regard to the first example given above, it may
be objected that the perceptual-political variables are already introduced into defense policy, for example, through State Department
interventions on such issues as U. S. troop deployments in Europe
and Korea and the deployment of the Sixth Fleet. (In regard to the
latter, the degree of detailed attention is such that consideration of
the possibility of withdrawing one of the two carriers in the Fleet
suffices to evoke strong State Department objections.) It is true
that in these established practices there are the rudiments of a
perceptual-political input for defense policy, but this is clearly

inadequate for it is confined to a very few issues, notably deployment decisions of particularly high visibility. There are no such inputs for force-structure planning or weapon-system procurement decisions, nor does it seem likely that agencies such as State or the International Security Affairs Office of the Defense Department would be qualified to provide detailed and continuing guidance on the perceptual-political dimension of these areas of decision.

CONCLUSION

It was argued above that it is not possible to extract the maximum politico-military benefit from the nation's expenditure on its military forces unless explicit consideration is given to the perceptual effects of their configuration, structure, and modes of deployment. It was further argued that it is well within the scope of the relevant disciplines and methods to evaluate such perceptual effects in a manner sufficiently unambiguous to allow the resulting data to be introduced in the decision-making processes of the Department of Defense. (This last proposition may be tested through case studies of perceptual-impact analyses of major decision alternatives.) It remains to devise procedures whereby the perceptual dimension of defense policy can be integrated within the established processes of decision; this last problem transcends the scope of the present study.

NOTES

1. See, for example, successive British Defence White Papers and U.S. "posture statements."
2. See R. J. Vincent, Military Power and Political Influence: The Soviet Union and Western Europe (London: International Institute for Strategic Studies, 1975) and Ken Booth, The Military Instrument in Soviet Foreign Policy, 1917-1972 (London: Royal United Services Institute for Defence Studies, 1974).
3. These particular figures come from the 1974-75 edition of Military Balance (London: IISS, 1974), p. 93. As the present writer has pointed out elsewhere [The US-USSR Nuclear Weapons Balance (Beverly Hills: Sage Publications, 1974), pp. 1-6.], most published assessments of the military balance are cast in terms of materiel or human inputs, and not in terms of the capability outputs. It is understood that output comparisons require the complex and uncertain evaluation of actual combat capabilities, while input comparisons are conceptually simple. This does not alter the fact that input comparisons

are sometimes quite meaningless, and almost always grossly
misleading.

    4. Detailed reference would be pointless. Among countless
examples official and otherwise, a recent ship-count statement is
quite remarkable. In the Philadelphia Enquirer, October 30, 1975
(p. 2B), Rear Admiral Wycliffe D. Toole, Jr., is reported as follows:
"Our Navy, today, has only 483 ships . . . . The Soviets now have
about 1,700 ships . . . that is gray-painted ships . . . . Some
experts have put the real strength of the Soviet Navy at closer to
2,200 ships."

3

THE MEASUREMENT OF WEAPONS-SYSTEM BALANCES: BUILDING UPON THE PERCEPTIONS OF EXPERTS

Edward J. Lawrence and
Ronald G. Sherwin

INTRODUCTION

This chapter is concerned with the problem of how one measures the capabilities of different countries relative to specific weapons systems (such as fighter aircraft or diesel attack submarines). After introducing and critiquing some methods currently employed, the writers suggest and illustrate the use of an alternative technique entailing multiple attribute utility (MAU) measurements. The technique explicitly incorporates the perceptions of relevant experts in assessing how different countries rank relative to a particular weapons systems balance.

CURRENT METHODS OF EVALUATING MILITARY BALANCES

We will briefly review current methods employed in evaluating military capability in order to establish a baseline from which to assess the utility of any new methods. One of the most commonly used measures is overall production costs,[1] the inference being that capability is related to these costs. A second method involves assigning dollar values to specific technical capabilities. The Stockholm International Peace Research Institute (SIPRI) utilizes such a method which values weapons systems by taking into account technological factors such as speed, pay load, and technological innovation, as well as production costs.[2] This method recognizes that the military capability of weapons—and the role they play in international relations—is not reflected in economic value alone.

A third approach, which we call the inventory approach, involves counting types of equipment such as tanks, fighter aircraft, or submarines in order to create a balance sheet. Those who construct such balance sheets often proceed to a somewhat higher level of measurement, incorporating in some way the performance characteristics of the weapons systems on the balance sheet. John Collins' Library of Congress study[3] provides a good example of this phenomenon. Referring to the disparity in the tactical airlift balance favoring the Soviet Union, he states that "this disparity is disproportionate, because nothing in the Soviet inventory matches the performance characteristics of the U.S. C-130 fleet, which is easily the world's best."[4]

A fourth approach is the formal aggregation of performance characteristics in order to assign quantitative values to specific weapons systems. This approach can employ the statistical technique of factor analysis, in which the characteristics of a weapons system such as an aircraft (speed, turning radius, thrust-to-weight ratio, maximum payload) are statistically combined to produce factors such as air superiority and ground support.[5] In another variant of this approach, ratio measures of capability are created by the simple product of speed, payload, and combat radius.[6] In a third variant, the Defense Intelligence Agency has developed a Theoretical Weapons Effectiveness score, a multiplicative index combining lethality (yield x rate of fire), accuracy (1/circular error probable), and survivability (reliability x mobility x vulnerability). Scores have been developed for over 200 Soviet weapons systems.[7]

CRITIQUE OF CURRENT METHODS

Although the above survey of current weapons-capability assessment techniques was necessarily brief,[8] it is complete enough to demonstrate some basic methodological weaknesses. First, there is very little attention paid to the validity and reliability of indicators. For example, SIPRI's valuation technique does not indicate the coding rules for assigning scores to weapons systems. The research cannot be replicated and hence lacks validity. A second problem involves the assumption in all of the methods that the indicators of military capability are linear. It is more likely that a weapons system will reach the "no value" point long before the indicators used reach zero. Also, the current methods do not take into account the law of diminishing returns or any other curvilinear function. A third weakness is the lack of attention paid to aggregation rules when multiple indicators of military capability are employed—does one add or multiply? A fourth issue can be termed the "balance-for-what-

purpose" problem. Most of the methods are not region- or mission-
specific. Despite the wide variety of methods, most can still be
categorized as "the baseball statistician's approach." It provides
the decision maker and analyst with a set of numbers but provides
little guidance as to how to use them to solve specific problems.
"Because the decision maker cannot understand or assimilate
thousands of numbers, all only indirectly related to the question at
hand, he has no choice but to select out a few, combine them with a
large dose of intuition and political savvy, and make a seat-of-the-
pants decision."[9]

Perhaps the most basic weakness of these methods is the total
lack of attention paid to the role of perceptions in evaluating military
capability. Analysts seek to explain deterrence and arms races using
dollar-valuation techniques without first demonstrating that nation-
states, in fact, react to money spent by both rivals and enemies.
Speed, payload, and combat radius are assumed to be the performance
characteristics which nation-states key on in making national-security
decisions. Much of this inadequacy is due to confusing actual combat
experience with quite different phenomena such as deterrence or
arms racing. Detailed analyses of battle outcomes may reveal the
importance of characteristics which might not be important when
used to explain an arms race. For example, U.S. analysts assessing
Latin American fighter-aircraft needs would probably conclude that
slow aircraft with maximum payloads would be most useful in likely
combat scenarios. Yet the Latin American preference is clearly for
fast, sleek fighters. What is needed is some method which can
incorporate this into an evaluation of capability. Only then can we
hope to understand and forecast the development, production, or
acquisition of military capability.

MULTIPLE-ATTRIBUTE UTILITY MEASUREMENT:
A STEP IN THE RIGHT DIRECTION

Faced with the above problems, particularly the problem of
incorporating perceptions, we have applied multiple-attribute utility
measurement (MAU) to measuring weapons system capability. The
basic idea of MAU measurement is that every outcome of an action
(in our case, the production or acquisition of military equipment) has
a value in a number of different dimensions. The technique involves
discovering these values, one dimension at a time, and then
aggregating them across dimensions using a suitable aggregation
rule and weighting procedure. Judges or experts are used to
determine both values and weights.[10] The technique involves a
clearly defined set of steps.

Step 1: Identify Issue for Study

For the purposes of demonstrating the method, we have
selected for assessment the sea-denial capability of attack submarines, and we will draw on data from a study by Lowell Jacoby. [11]
Two different scenarios apply: (1) guerilla-type attacks by submarines
against either merchant ships or nonmissile surface combatants; and
(2) a war-at-sea scenario. In both scenarios, it is assumed that the
surface unit was alert to the possibility of attack but lacked airborne
ASW (antisubmarine warfare) support. The main point in spelling
out these scenarios is to make the evaluation of weapons systems
realistic by relating their capability to a particular scenario.

Step 2: Identify Entities to be Evaluated

Torpedo-firing diesel submarines are the entities being
evaluated.

Step 3: Identify the Relevant Dimensions
of Value for Evaluation of the Entities

What are the components of sea denial (submarines) which
define their military worth? As polled by Jacoby, U. S. naval experts
have agreed on the following list of dimensions for submarines:

Submerged Displacement	Number of Torpedoes
Submerged Speed	Torpedo Guidance Systems
Submerged Endurance	Acquistion Techniques
Number of Torpedo Tubes	ESM (electronic support measures) Capability
Torpedo Speed	SLAM (submarine launched anti-ship missile) Capability
Effective Range of Torpedo	Capability of County to Operate Equipment

Step 4: Weight Dimension

Using Delphi or any other aggregating technique, [12] agreement
must be reached regarding the rank and weight of the above

components in contribution to the total military worth of the system. This is the heart of the MAU approach.

> Arguments over public policy typically turn out to hinge on disagreements about values. Normally such disagreements are fought out in the context of specific decisions, over and over again, at enormous social cost each time a decision must be made. Multiple-attribute utility measurement can spell out explicitly what the values of each participant (decision maker, expert, pressure group, government, etc.) are, show how and how much they differ. By explicitly negotiating about, agreeing on and (if appropriate) publicizing a set of values, a decision-making organization can, in effect, inform those affected by its decisions about its ground rules. [13]

The dimensions must be weighted while preserving ratios. The least important characteristic is assigned a score of 1, with subsequent characteristics weighted by asking how much more important (if at all) is it than the least important? The mean importance weight for each characteristic is then calculated. Some examples from the Jacoby study are listed below. They represent submarine weightings for scenario 1.

Dimension	Average Weighting	Standard Deviation
Submerged Displacement	3.3	2.80
Submerged Speed	4.7	1.51
Number of Torpedo Tubes	4.0	3.63
Torpedo Speed	6.3	1.97
Effective Range of Torpedo	6.2	2.14
Acquistion Techniques	7.3	1.75

These weightings point out some of the characteristics of MAU. First, it is apparent that you can get judges (in this case n=6) to discriminate among dimensions. Second, the level of agreement varies considerably, as evidenced by the standard deviations.

Step 5: Judges Construct Utility Curves for Each Dimension

The judges are now asked to draw a graph (Figure 3.1). The X-axis of each graph represents the plausible range of performance

FIGURE 3.1

Submerged Speed: Scenario #1

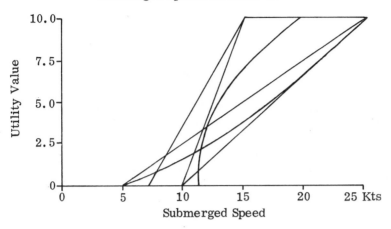

Source: Compiled by the author.

values for the dimension-characteristic under consideration. The
Y-axis represents the utilities (1-10) associated with the corresponding X-values. This is the second crucial aspect of MAU. Recall
that one of the major problems with current measurement schemes
is the assumption of linearity. At this step in the MAU procedure,
the researcher has an opportunity to empirically determine the
shape of the characteristic's contribution to the military worth of the
entity/weapons system being evaluated. Shown below is a curve
submitted by judges for the characteristic "Submerged Speed" in
evaluating its contribution to the sea denial capability of a submarine.

There are two aspects of this curve-drawing procedure which
need elaboration. First, there is the point of zero utility. It is
obviously possible either to force a consensus using a Delphi
approach, or report the lack of consensus in terms of a mean and
standard deviation. If the above curve was the first iteration, a new
consensus curve with the mean speed of 8.1 knots representing
zero utility would be suggested as the group solution. The second
part of the curve which is of interest is the maximum-utility point.
Here you ask the judge at what point will more of a certain characteristic not add any more capability for the scenario under discussion.

Step 6: Aggregate Utility Curves

Edwards et al. reviewed the literature concerning the problems
involved in aggregating individual utilities into group-utility functions.

They concluded that averaging presented an acceptable method for resolving disagreement among judges. [14] Given this conclusion, there are two ways to average the curves. First, as previously mentioned, some sort of Delphi technique can be used to produce one consensus curve for each characteristic.

The second approach includes using the judges' utility curves directly to average the values for each dimension. In the "Submerged Speed" curve previously shown, a submarine with a submerged speed of 10 knots would receive a utility score of [0. 0 + 0. 0 + 0. 0 + 1. 5 + 2. 5 + 3. 8)/6 =] 1. 3. It is necessary to take six individual utility readings, sum them, and divide by the number of judges.

Step 7: Calculate Entity/Weapon System Utilities

At this point in the process, the analyst marries the results of Step 6 (utilities for each dimension) with those of Step 4 (weights for each dimension). This is also the most hazardous step methodologically, since the analyst must decide how to combine the dimensions—addition or multiplication. Although the theory behind aggregation is rather complex, [15] we will briefly describe the issues involved. If we simply add the dimensions to come up with a score for a submarine, we assume that if one of the dimensions is zero (for example, for torpedo speed), it can be compensated for by a high value on another dimension. In a theoretical sense, therefore, very few weapons systems could be evaluated using the additive rule. In reality, however, weapons systems rarely are produced with a total lack of value on a dimension, thus allowing us to use the additive rule in most cases. For the submarine study, the weighted utilities of all the sea-denial components of submarines were added, producing the following selected results. (Maximum score is 20. 00.)

Scenario #1		Scenario #2	
Guppy III SS	20. 00	Type 209 SS	19. 75
Foxtrot SS	15. 42	Oberon SS	18. 18
Type 209 SS	15. 38	Foxtrot SS	17. 44
Oberon	14. 78	Guppy III SS	17. 23
Tiburon	10. 24	Tiburon SS	9. 59

Note that the judges have been able to discriminate between scenarios. In the sneak-attack scenario, a Guppy III SS has a maximum amount of capability but is definitely less capable against greater opposition. The opposite is true of the German 209, which fares much better in an open-sea environment.

Step 8: Integrate Human Factors

Probably the most frequent criticism of quantitative approaches to valuating a weapons system is that the system's value will depend on terrain, tactics, and operator-proficiency. Hence the effort at combat modeling. However, it is the assumption of this research that decision makers key on a few basic variables. One of these is the ability of a nation to operate the equipment. It became quickly apparent that the MAU technique could not be applied in this case, since there were no indicators such as speed, turning radius, and so on which could be applied to questions of competence of operator, maintenance proficiency, logistics, etc. The search for an alternative method was constrained by the fact that it had to produce ratio-level data which could be mathematically combined with the platform utility scores developed in Step 8.

The method selected was the constant-sum method. [16] The method calls upon the judge to consider every possible pair of antagonists. Within each pair, the judge is asked to divide 100 points between the two instances in accordance with the absolute ratio of the greater to the lesser. The judges in the sea-denial study were asked to evaluate a specific country's capability to successfully operate torpedo-firing diesel submarines in an open-sea denial mission. The instructions suggested that evaluations might be based in part on a demonstrated capability to perform the open-ocean mission, the presence of the technology and training necessary for successful accomplishment of the mission, and the ability of a particular nation to man the platforms with competent crews. The purpose of the suggestions was to focus the judge's attention on an evaluation of the personnel factors.

A judge who evaluated Egypt and Syria with a 50:50 score is saying that their personnel capability is equal. If another judge rates Israel-Tunisia 80:20, he is saying that Israel's navy personnel are four times as capable as Tunisia's. The aggregation technique used to go from the individual splits to a ratio scale is straightforward, but lengthy, so the reader is referred to Torgerson's Theory and Methods of Scaling. [17] Some examples of the scores produced by this method are listed below. They have been transformed to a scale of 0-20 to match the previously shown submarine scale.

Israel	20.00	North Korea	10.59
PRC	15.34	South Korea	8.33
Iran	14.26	Iraq	5.87
South Africa	12.34	Saudi Arabia	5.03
Egypt	12.28	Tunisia	2.82
India	11.56	Ivory Coast	1.50

The judges have one final task, that of assessing the relative importance of human-versus-equipment factors for each of the scenarios. In the case of the diesel submarines, the factors were judged to be roughly equivalent. The total score, therefore, for an Iranian 209 SS in scenario 2 is 14. 26 + 19. 75 = 34. 01. The same submarine in Iraqi hands has a value of 5. 87 + 19. 75 = 25. 62.

Step 9: Assign Country-Capability Score

The final step in the process is to produce a country score. In our above example, the value of 34. 01 calculated for an Iranian 209 SS submarine is multiplied times the number in service. It is here that the value of creating ratio-level data is appreciated, since this final step can only be taken with ratio data. Excerpted below are some examples of country scores for scenario 2 sea-denial capability, evaluating only submarines.

Turkey	3297	Peru	1394
North Korea	3006	Pakistan	600
Egypt	2935	Taiwan	459
India	2111	Chile	433
PRC	1646	Israel	294
Greece	1511	South Korea	0

AN ASSESSMENT OF THE MAU APPROACH

As the reader has most likely concluded, there is much more to the MAU technique than has been summarized here. However, assuming that this brief introduction to MAU has been sufficient, we now return to our original set of problems in order to assess whether in fact MAU is a step in the right direction.

Briefly reviewing our critique of current methods, we can see that MAU directly addresses the questions of data validity and reliability. An indicator of military capability is said to be valid if it is an "adequate measure of what it is supposed to represent. " We are also told that "concepts are judged not by their truth or falsity, but by their theoretical utility. " It is apparent that this "validity" is greatly influenced by the perceptions of those using it. Data reliability is even more related to perceptions, since it concerns whether or not an indicator of military balance "yields results that are consistent in successive measurements of the same case. " Do successive observers, looking at the same phenomenon, all see the same thing? By explicitly involving decision makers (or their

analysts) in the construction of the indicators of capability, valid and
reliable indicators are much more likely to emerge.

The second problem—that of linearity—is overcome in that MAU
gives the judges an opportunity to depict curvilinear relationships if
they exist. Third, although we did not go into it in great detail in this
chapter, MAU quite explicitly addresses the problem of how to
aggregate the dimensions of military capability. And fourth, the
technique clearly focuses on the balance associated with the use of a
specific type of hardware in a mission-oriented scenario. It does not
focus on general balances such as the overall naval balance.

By far, the biggest contribution MAU has made to the process
of evaluating military capability is its explicit incorporation of
perceptions. To highlight these contributions, we refer to Luttwak's
chapter in this book in which he outlines several problems encountered
when nontechnical observers assess military balances. In essence,
these problems result from not considering perceptions. Does the
MAU technique alleviate any of these problems?

Luttwak points out that force-level figures are readily absorbed
because numbers are conceptually simple in themselves. MAU is
particularly susceptible to misuse on this account. Numbers have a
way of being locked in once they are calculated. For example, will
the personnel score for Saudi Arabia be changed as their performance improves? It will, but only if the judges' opinions are tapped
on a systematic basis. It is also prudent to build into any data-
analysis system based on MAU a range of values, so that analysts
can conduct sensitivity tests with their indicators.

Luttwak also talks about numbers requiring a context. The
scenario-specific aspect of our example contronts this problem
directly. A third issue was raised which concerns the fact that
individual numbers are readily absorbed but an accumulation of
numbers may not be. This is a problem that can be readily solved
with a data-retrieval and display system capable of taking basic MAU
findings, storing them, and trending the balances over time. The
fourth issue is that performance data are readily absorbed, but only
if a clearly understood index of normality is provided. MAU specifically provides an opportunity for the decision makers (or their analysts)
who are charged with computing capability to provide such an index,
i. e. , during the construction of the weights and utility curves. The
judges are specifically asked to show at what point a weapons system
has zero utility. More importantly, this is a psychic baseline
reflecting the multitude of variables being processed by the human
brain.

Luttwak also refers to the problem of qualitative information
being absorbed only if it can be conveyed in visual terms or in verbal
imagery. The constant-sum approach, used to calculate country

personnel scores in our study, relies heavily on verbal imagery. In many cases, the judge will have worked with foreign navies, read intelligence reports, etc. —all of which contribute to the image he has of a country's naval personnel. It was the one step in the process where the components of the attribute could not be disaggregated, and the total image was relied on.

Luttwak's last two observations are the most relevant to MAU. He hypothesizes that personal experience of the reality of on-going military activities may have a wholly disproportionate impact on perceptions of military capabilities. This is clearly a danger for MAU in that judges may be biased in this regard. On the other hand, MAU forces the judge to look at all of the components of a particular system, one at a time, thereby increasing the probability that a U.S. naval-pilot judge will not underestimate Soviet anticarrier capabilities. And, finally, there is the problem of nontechnical observers giving greater value to technologically advanced features in military equipments than is warranted by their actual contribution to force-effectiveness. In a sense, the MAU technique is neutral regarding this problem, since all the technique can do is make clear the preferences of the judges. If a Peruvian air force officer heavily judges weight, speed, and sleekness in evaluating fighter-aircraft capability, so be it. The advantage is that these biases are in the open and can be taken into account.

Overall, the MAU technique appears to solve many of the problems involved when perceptions are not considered. In addition, the technique explicitly recognizes that human experience and analytical capabilities cannot be duplicated by a machine. MAU builds on these human judgments. On a related point, human analysts who serve as experts constantly update their knowledge. Any data system which periodically taps this knowledge automatically updates itself in a fashion impossible to duplicate.

The flexibility of the technique should also be mentioned. If your judgment-based balance proves to be in error (e.g., your calculated imbalance caused you to react in a fashion that was counter-productive), you have an explicit record of how the faulty balance was calculated. Such a system forces the decision maker to look at which analysts were on the mark and for what reasons. It tells you how much of a consensus you have among your experts regarding a specific balance. MAU allows the decision maker to close the feedback loop. Do perceptions match reality? For example, did the increase in sea-denial capability of country X really force rival country Y to acquire the same, as your experts predicted?

PROBLEM AREAS AND FUTURE RESEARCH

There are certain questions that have been raised in regard to applying the MAU technique to the evaluation of military capabilities, the answers to which serve to highlight the strengths, weaknesses, and potential of the method. First, there are a host of technical questions, particularly regarding the aggregation rules. The key problem for those using the method is those weapons systems with extreme values on a particular dimension. To this point, MAU has been used for the sea-denial and air-superiority missions. Further work on other missions and weapons systems will be required before these technical problems are solved.

A second set of questions revolves around the selection and availability of experts. If a method relies totally on expert judgment, such a problem is not trivial. If one is concerned with an objective, technical statement of the military balance, the problem indeed exists. However, if we assume that balances are constructed and utilized by policy-making organizations, the MAU approach is more useful. The guiding principle here is that the policy makers will task clearly defined groups of experts, normally from their own organizations. One only has to look at the varying estimates of the Soviet navy within the U. S. government to see this phenomenon at work. This approach is obviously well suited to the bureaucratic-politics model of policy making. There is no "objective" version of the balance, only various organizational versions. Therefore, the problem of using the best judges is much easier to solve.

A third aspect of the MAU technique which some have questioned is the idea that the overall capability of a weapons system cannot be evaluated in a rigorous sense without disaggregating it into capability dimensions. We have conducted a significant amount of tests which show that experts can reliably rank-order specific aircraft and ships as to capability. However, the multidimensional aspect of modern weapons systems does not allow the expert to evaluate how much more capable one system is than another. There are methods available to translate rank-order data into interval-level data. But as we have seen, the key to calculating country-capability scores is creating a ratio score for a weapons system which can then be multiplied by the number in the inventory. In a sense, there is a dilemma. On one hand, MAU assumes that the whole is equal to the sum of its parts, an assumption which does not completely capture the essence of a weapons system. On the other hand, a weapons system is too complex to evaluate it holistically without running into the perceptual biases mentioned earlier.

Finally, it must be stated that MAU is a method reserved for specific weapons balances. In no way should the method be used to construct a total military-capability score for a country. The most we can expect from such a method is a series of balances analogous to the various dials and meters on an aircraft. Each dial, in our case a mission-specific balance, represents an accurate reading, but only the pilot or the policy maker can combine them for a net assessment of the overall situation. The fact that such a new assessment may be fraught with errors and biases does not detract from the necessity to construct valid and reliable weapons-balance estimates which incorporate perceptions.

NOTES

1. Jonathan Wilkenfeld et al. , "Conflict Interactions in the Middle East, 1949-1967," Journal of Conflict Resolution 16 (1972): 135-54; Robert Burrowes and J. Garriga-Pico, "One Road to the Six Day War: Rational Analysis of Conflict and Cooperation," Peace Science Society Papers 22 (1974): 47-74; and J. M. McCormick, "Evaluating Models of Crisis Behavior: Some Evidence from the Middle East," International Studies Quarterly 19 (1975); 17-45.

2. Stockholm International Peace Research Institute, Arms Trade with the Third World (New York: Humanities Press, 1971).

3. John Collins, United States/Soviet Military Balance: A Frame of Reference for Congress (Washington, D.C.: U.S. Government Printing Office, 1976).

4. Ibid. , p. 14.

5. Lewis Snider, Middle East Maelstrom: The Impact of Global and Regional Influences on the Arab-Israeli Conflict: 1947-1973 (Ph.D. Dissertation, University of Michigan, 1975); and Alan Legrow, Measuring Aircraft Capability for Military and Political Analysis (Master's Thesis, Naval Postgraduate School, March 1976).

6. Hans Rattinger, "From War to War: Arms Races in the Middle East," International Studies Quarterly 20 (December 1976): 501-31.

7. Consolidated Analysis Corporation, Inc. , Developmental Methodologies for Medium to Long-Range Estimates: Users Manual for Soviet Effectiveness Model (Washington: CACI, September 1976).

8. For a more complete assessment of these methods, see Edward J. Laurance, "The International Transfer of Arms: Problems of Measurement and Conceptualization" (Paper presented at the 1977 Annual Meeting of the Midwest Political Science Association, Chicago, April 1977).

9. Ward Edwards et al. , "A Decision-Theoretic Approach to Evaluation Research," in Elmer Struening and Marcia Guttenteg, eds. , Handbook of Evaluation Research, vol. 1 (Beverly Hills: Sage Publications, 1975), p. 147.

10. See ibid. for the basic methodology. Also see Ward Edwards, How to Use Multi-Attribute Utility Measurement for Social Decision-Making (Los Angeles: Social Science Research Institute, University of Southern California, August 1976).

11. See Lowell Jacoby, Quantitative Assessment of Third World Sea-Denial Capabilities, (Master's Thesis, Naval Postgraduate School, March 1977).

12. Delphi is a method in which judges estimate values as individuals, the responses are collated and summarized, and then sent back to the judges. The judges again estimate values. Iterations continue until either a consensus value or a well-described split emerges. For a good summary and critique of the method, see Oskar Morgenstern et al. , Long Term Projections of Power: Political, Economic and Military Forecasting (Cambridge: Ballinger, 1973).

13. See Edwards, op. cit. , and Laurance, op. cit.

14. Ibid.

15. Ibid.

16. Warren S. Torgerson, Theory and Methods of Scaling (New York: John Wiley & Sons, Inc. , 1958).

17. Ibid.

PART
2

EVIDENCE AND
CASE STUDIES

4

THE STATUS AND SIGNIFICANCE
OF THE SUPERPOWER STRATEGIC
BALANCE: DIFFERING AMERICAN VIEWS

Senator John Culver and twenty-two other senators of both parties sponsored a unique gathering of some of the well-known participants in the ongoing debate over U. S. security policies. The congressional conference was held on May 11-12, 1977, in the Caucus Room of the U. S. Senate. The Honorable Stuart Symington returned to the Senate for the first time since his retirement to moderate a wide-ranging discussion that focused on defense priorities and prescriptions for the next quarter-century. The twenty-three panelists, not all of whom are quoted here, represented a thorough mix of professional experiences and points of view. Their opening remarks, in which they assess the superpower balance as well as what they see as important strategic trends, are excerpted below.

SENATOR JOHN CULVER: Seldom in our history has the United States faced such crucial decisions about national security policy, decisions with such far-reaching consequences. We have emerged from one war in Southeast Asia with no clear national consensus other than to avoid a repetition of that particular kind of conflict. We are facing a rapidly changing world in which many of our long-established ideas and approaches are being challenged by new constellations of problems and forces.

Originally published as "Documentation: U. S. National Security—1977-2001," International Security, II, 2 (Fall, 1977), pp. 171-83. Excerpted here with the permission of the President and Fellows of Harvard College.

In assembling this distinguished panel, every effort has been made to get the best exposition possible of differing opinions in the wide spectrum of national defense philosophy. Only by considering all sides of these issues can we hope to attain insight and overview.

PAUL NITZE   (Chairman of Policy Studies of the Committee on the Present Danger; former Under Secretary of Defense, Secretary of the Navy, and U.S. SALT Delegate): It seems to me that one must look at the problem [of national defense] as being twofold—what one can achieve through arms control and then what is necessary to add through our own defense program. The intention is that the total of what one gets through arms control, plus one's own weapon development program, results in balance and in a maintenance of crisis stability. I think this is important to the peace of the world and important to our defense—simply an important foundation for the conduct of U.S. foreign policy.

The question has been asked, "What is the status of the United States' ability to defend itself against attack in the 1977-1985 period?" I would consider that to be a misformulation of the problem. I do not believe that the Soviet Union wants war. I believe they intend to accomplish their objectives without war, if possible. I think it is important that there be a balance and that we maintain crisis stability through the combination of arms control and of the defenses which we ourselves deploy.

RAY CLINE   (Executive Director of Studies at Georgetown University Center for Strategic and International Studies; former Deputy Director of the CIA and Director of Intelligence and Research at the State Department): I think Secretary Nitze is correct in saying that the danger that confronts this country in the period we are talking about is not that the USSR will decide to rain nuclear bombs on this country or even on our allies in Western Europe. The danger is that the Soviet Union intends to continue to change the global balance of power—military, economic, and political—in a direction unfavorable to the United States. It seems to me that they have been fairly successful in starting trends in that direction which, if continued into the 1985 period, will leave us in a much diminished position of power and influence. In a sense, we are like decaying gentility, facing adverse circumstances without deciding what to do about them.

I think the real dilemma that confronts this country is that we had a period of exceptional strategic good fortune in which our political, economic, and military links to important nations around the world—nations that wanted our friendship, wanted our cooperation, and above all, did not wish to be dominated by any totalitarian power, particularly not by the Soviet Union—chose to work with us and strengthened our influence in diplomatic and strategic affairs. The alliance system is what is threatened today, because of the growing feeling that the Soviet Union is on a dynamic upward course in all of the aspects of national power—not just the military aspect—and that the United States is not very clear about what it should do in the face of that kind of challenge.

It seems clear to me that the key factors in international power and influence have to do with the intangibles more than with the concrete military and economic facts of life. Those intangibles are a sense of clear and coherent national purpose, a strategy for the country in its interests and national affairs, and, above all, a coherence of political will—a political determination to protect the nation and to carry out its strategy, whatever it may be.

HERBERT SCOVILLE (Secretary of the Arms Control Association; former Deputy Director of the CIA): I do not believe that the strategic balance is as delicate at the moment as some would have us believe. In fact, I think both superpowers have such large strategic forces that any changes that can occur in a short period of time will not seriously alter that balance at all. Secondly, I think that the strategic balance is very stable at the moment. There is no threat that either side can destroy a significant portion of the deterrents of the other side.

On the other hand, this situation may not last very long—not that the deterrent as a whole is going to be eroded, because there is no visible threat to the submarine—for there is an increasing threat to the land-based ICBM part of our force. It is the new weapon programs on the part of both the Soviet Union and ourselves which, over a period of time, will decrease this stability. The development of MIRV, heavy ICBMs with improved accuracies on the part of the Soviet Union, the MX, and the Mark 12-A warhead for the Minute Man III are all examples of destabilizing technology.

I think we are much stronger than perhaps the general public has any concept of. I do not agree with Ray Cline that the trend is all that disturbingly against us. Not only have we in the last five years increased the sizes of our strategic forces at a more rapid rate than has the Soviet Union, but I do not see any sign that that is particularly changing.

It is true that we are now finishing our MIRV programs while the Soviet Union is just starting theirs. But we have programs for a whole series of new-generation strategic weapons which will still further increase the war-making potential of our strategic forces. So I see nothing to indicate that we won't continue to have an advantage, although I find this advantage somewhat mythical and not very practical since neither side can use these forces anyway.

The security of all of us would be much better off if, instead of these buildups on both sides, we went to arms-control measures, particularly those arms-control measures which would affect the qualitative race. Numbers don't make much difference anymore; the real threat is with new types of weapons.

FRED WARNER NEAL (Chairman of the International Relations Faculty at Claremont Graduate School; Chairman of the Executive Committee on U. S. -Soviet Relations): It seems to me that our discussion can only be meaningful if it is placed in the overall American foreign policy context, especially with reference to overall American policy towards the Soviet Union.

So far as the hardware is concerned and so far as the Soviet military buildup is concerned, there is, of course, a wide opinion in the United States that the Soviet Union is ahead of us in certain categories. What is more significant, I think, is what the perception is in Moscow. I don't think the perception in Moscow is like that at all. The Soviet Union for a great many years has very much been behind the United States in all weapon categories. What it has been doing for a decade, at least as used to be said in trotting races, is coming up fast on the outside. They won't stop—short of some kind of international agreement—and perhaps not even then, because of a suspicion that the Americans will keep going ahead. And the Americans will not refrain from going ahead because of a suspicion that, if the Russians do achieve what they think is equality, they won't stop.

EARL RAVENAL (Adjunct Professor of American Foreign Policy, SAIS, Johns Hopkins; former Department of Defense official): I would agree with Paul Nitze's statement that we should consider in conjunction the question of arms control and the question of the unilateral policies that we apply to the design of our forces. To a large extent the objectives of arms control are the same as the objectives toward which we design our strategic forces.

I don't have any doubt that some kind of a mutually agreeable arrangement will be worked out between the United States and the Soviet Union, roughly within the time limits of the present interim agreement and roughly within the parameters of the October 1976 version of the accords of November 1974—that is, the modifications of numbers and the possible remedies for the current stalemate over the Soviet Backfire bomber and the American cruise-missile programs.

But I think it ought to be recognized that such an agreement will not satisfy nearly all American strategic thinkers on the issue of strategic stability. There will still be contention and arguments that

the Soviets will be capable within these negotiated limits of building
the kinds of forces that might be, in a crisis, capable of destabilizing
the strategic balance. And I think that the arguments of those who
take this pessimistic view should not be ignored. I think they have to
be countered, and they have to be countered not only in words, but by
a program of supplementary American moves, unilateral if necessary,
to reestablish the balance.

We can tailor our forces in the direction of reestablishing and
ensuring strategic stability, but we can do it on the down side. We
can do it with fewer weapons and less of a force. In the case of
strategic arms competition, less is not less, less can be more. But
less certainly can be enough.

WILLIAM F. COLBY (Former Director of the Central Intelligence
Agency): I think the subject of our strategic power must be looked at
without a myopia. This is a problem that our country has had in many
situations where we focus on only one problem of the strategic
situation. The most outrageous example of that was when we focused
on the military aspect of the Vietnam War and made a mistake of
ignoring for many years the political and guerrilla aspects. When
we look at the strategic balance in the world today, we should not
only look at the large weapons systems that we and the Soviets con-
front each other with, but we also need to look at the conventional
weapons and the many other problems that we have. Our most serious
threats today probably are in Western Europe on the conventional
level—conventional threats which we for years have thought to meet
by going to nuclear warfare on the tactical level.

Furthermore, I believe that there are real strategic problems
ahead, and that we have to put the fact of the imbalance of economics
and of social good in the world into our equation when we think of
strategic security. Indeed, we can spend great sums of money
matching large Soviet weapons, and ignore the sums that would be
necessary to match Soviet conventional force. But expenditures must
also be used to conduct positive political and economic programs with
respect to that three-quarters of the earth's humanity that lives in
the third world so that we can get these peoples of the world to be
our friends instead of our enemies. Indeed, such underdevelopment
is the most dangerous problem we have. We cannot look upon our
own budgetary problems as an argument to support how little we are
spending on economic programs and assistance and trade relations
with these parts of the world. By worrying only about strategic
weapons we will indeed be fighting the wrong war. We need to avoid
another myopia in which we focus on a numbers balance in weapons,
and instead turn to a consideration of what is sufficient to meet the
threat—the threat in the super weapons, the threat in the conventional

weapons, but also the threat in terms of economic and political chaos around the world.

CHARLES YOST (Aspen Institute Program in Communication and Society; former U. S. Ambassador to the United Nations): I am happy to note that there seems to be general agreement that the Soviet Union is unlikely to initiate a direct attack upon us. As Mr. Scoville has pointed out, the size and character of our arsenal is such that strategic deterrence cannot be croded or shortened in a space of time, particularly our submarine-based deterrent.

Well, if this is so, what is the major threat? I don't always agree with Henry Kissinger, but I would like to read one sentence from a statement he made just before he left the State Department. He said, "I would say that if there is a conflict between the Soviet Union and us, it is much less likely to occur as a result of a Soviet attack than as a result of a conflict that maybe neither of us foresaw, under which we were drawn through a series of escalating moves."

In other words, I think World War I is a better guide to our current dangers than World War II. If that is correct, I would suspect that our major danger is one that has been referred to by several of the speakers, competion in the third world; these 100 new states where the escalating, competitive moves by both superpowers could lead us into a war that neither has planned nor wanted. One of our central security concerns should be to find means of restraining and controlling this competition. The danger arises from the Soviets attempting to upset in some of these critical third would areas what they see as an unfavorable situation. And there I feel that we should engage in a much more serious negotiation with them in order to avoid this eventuality. As Mr. Colby suggests, we should concentrate on putting more of our resources on strengthening countries themselves so that they are much less susceptible to foreign exploitation.

REAR ADMIRAL GENE LA ROCQUE, USN, Ret. (Director, Center for Defense Information): Several times the term "military balance" has come up. I don't think that there is such a thing as a military balance. It is the military imbalance, and it is disequilibrium, it is instability; the military on both sides cannot live with a balance. The job of the military is to win, and I think we ought to take that into account as we deliberate. Unfortunately, though, if you use the term "military balance," and it is current today, you can persuade the American people that if you just put a little more weight on our side it will bring things into our favor, and then we are all going to be safe. But the U. S. has been ahead of the Soviet Union by at least five years in the development of every major strategic weapons system.

Apropos of the SALT talks, I think if we look realistically at
the ones that have taken place, none of them have really significantly
increased our national defense or our national security. That is not
to say that we ought not to continue them, but basically we are less
secure after the SALT agreements than we were before we started.
We are less secure today with the more money we spend and the more
weapons systems we develop than we were before we undertook them.

I think we could take some very positive initiatives, and sober
initiatives, in recognition of the fact that we can destroy all life on
this planet. Just about three months ago China tested one nuclear
weapon, and the people in Philadelphia and Baltimore were told to
stay inside and wash their vegetables. One nuclear weapon. We are
talking about unleashing some 20,000 strategic nuclear weapons, and
if we use all of our tactical force as well, we are talking of 50,000
nuclear weapons, so that it is not a matter of hiding in the ground
for a little while; we are talking about destroying all life on this
planet.

I think the United States ought to suggest and agree to stop
testing nuclear weapons for a period of two years. It wouldn't hurt
us a bit. I think we ought to stop building more nuclear weapons
for a period of two years. Simply stop spending more each year for
our military budget.

LT. GEN. ROYAL ALLISON, USAF, Ret. (Consultant on oil and
energy; former United States SALT Delegate): When we were engaged
in the SALT negotiations, I was asked rather frequently during the
period that we were here in Washington as to why I thought the Soviets
wish to negotiate with us on strategic arms. After the first and second
sessions, it seems to me that the Soviets wanted to negotiate a
position that would be publicly looked upon as one of strategic equality
with the United States. That kind of strategic equality is purely a
matter of perception. We must be sure that we perceive our own
strengths correctly, that we perceive the Soviet strengths as
correctly as we can, and when we consider our own strength we do
not do it by counting comparative weapon systems and fatalities.
Those kinds of evaluations can be very misleading.

I want to make some more specific comments on weapons and
negotiations. I will do it in the reverse order, because I think we are
strong. The United States should not fear to negotiate at any time at
any place with anyone. When we started the SALT negotiations we
considered—I considered, and I believe those of us with whom I was
working considered—it a first step in a long, long haul. We were
going to have to have patience. We should not expect an immediate
solution. There were no quick answers to these things. Sometimes

as I read what is written these days, I wonder if these commentators remember how difficult it was to get the negotiations started, and that when they were started we were saying to ourselves just what I am saying now, that we are in this for a very long haul.

Now the second thing on weapons—numbers are not the sole answer. I believe very deeply, however, that one of the most important offsetting factors for the United States is our technology, our scientific ability, our research and development—essentially the ability that we have proved over the years to do the very nearly impossible. We have had men walk on the moon, for example, and no one else has. So when we talk about weaponry and numbers, I suggest that we should always reserve to ourselves the right to let the minds of men create what the minds of men will create. We don't stand the chance of a snowball in a hot place of verifying qualitative controls on technology. This being the case, we should think long and hard before we forego the right to develop ourselves the things that we know we can, and we believe the other fellow might develop if he had time.

JOHN STEINBRUNER (Associate Professor of Political Science, Yale University; Editorial Board Member, International Security): Let me underline a few things which I think are going to become of great importance over the period we have been talking about. We live in a world in which political crisis appears to be academic. It will require different conceptual ideas to master the many issues in this area having to do with command and control. Exercising intelligent military command over far-flung, very extensive military forces with peculiar vulnerabilities requires far more study. We really have got to put this at the center of our defense planning and we have not done so.

The second point I would try to underline is that I think we ought to recognize that we have a very bad history in interpreting the Soviet Union. We have been wrong about them in their strategic programs and in important respects since the mid-1960s. These errors come about for honest reasons. The Soviets are very difficult to read. They don't tell us as much as we would like to know. Yet it is becoming increasingly important that we get it right.

So I believe that one of the most important strategic problems of the future is simply better intelligence analysis of the enemy. We have been very casual and somewhat ideological in this respect for a number of years, and I think we have to get much more sophisticated about understanding the enemy that we definitely have.

COL. JOHN COLLINS, USA, Ret. (Senior Specialist in National Defense, Congressional Research Service of the Library of Congress):

It is pretty clear to me that increasing Soviet capabilities across the board, not just strategic-nuclear capabilities, leave the United States less secure than it was a few years ago. I would suggest to you all, as an example, that essential equivalence is the poorest possible force-structure standard that the United States could use in approaching the SALT table. It clouds our true requirements. It causes us to react to Soviet holdings rather than to our own needs. It causes us to buy things we don't need and at the same time to slight the things we do.

I can guarantee to you that there is no way to reverse that trend until we find some way to identify our true requirements. That is not going to happen until we can relate all of these forces and funds to an agreed foreign policy, which we do not have today, and until we can relate all of these forces and funds to a sound military strategy, which we do not have today—in fact, we don't even have an effective way to formulate conceptual strategy in the United States. It is certainly not being done in the Department of Defense. It is not being done in the Joint Chiefs of Staff. It is not being done in any of the military services. You think perhaps that the National Security Council is going to pull all this together, that this is where the conceptual planning takes place. I can tell you that that is false.

The National Security Council is geared to crisis management, not to conceptual planning. I would like to tell everybody that will listen to me that strategy is like research and development. It has two pieces. One piece is called basic scientific research, and the other is called applied technology. In the field of strategy, there isn't anybody in the United States, to my knowledge, who is really on the basic scientific research side. Everybody who thinks he is playing strategy in this country is on the applied technology side, and as a result the decision makers at the top levels of your government are playing with strategic concepts that were put together 10 or 15 years ago to satisfy requirements which have long since disappeared.

You can spend this Treasury dry without insuring better security unless you find some effective way to relate forces and funds back to strategy and foreign policy. That is my message.

LT. GEN. DANIEL GRAHAM, USA, Ret. (Professor of Advanced International Studies, University of Miami; former Director of the Defense Intelligence Agency): Those who believe that strategic equivalence and parity is a reasonable point of view for the United States forget one thing, and that is that our society demands that in all of our military planning we yield the initiative to our adversary, because we cannot base our forces on the proposition that we will attack or launch aggression against our major adversary. Any military man can tell you that parity plus initiative is superiority.

In the last six or eight years the curve for the United States has been generally downward. I would take it that Dr. Scoville was talking about having more individual warheads or something. But if you take the general trends in those same capabilities that have been downward for the United States, upward for the Soviet Union, at some point the lines either have crossed, are crossing, or will cross. That is the important matter, not what the precision of the balance is today.

DEREK LEEBAERT (Research Fellow, Harvard University; Managing Editor, International Security): Discussion of military power and the superpower balance—or imbalance—could not be more timely. This administration has brought a new dynamic to the development and deployment of nuclear as well as conventional weapons. But what remains to be considered for the coming quarter-century is how this power will be translated into international influence in a time of decreasing military utility.

We not only have to question what we actually mean by "security," but we must appreciate that traditional global military assessments are becoming increasingly anachronistic. One thinks of NATO as it approaches its thirtieth anniversary. In this case alliance cohesion is far less threatened by external military aggression than by internal disarray. Economic, political, and sociological concerns have become integral parts of any defense calculus.

Perhaps the most provocative part of any security-related prognosis is the new distribution of both defense expenditures and the proclivities to use force. According to ACDA [Arms Control and Disarmament Agency], military outlays for NATO, the Warsaw Pact, and the less developed countries rose 23, 29, and 100 percent respectively. Other indicators, such as defense spending as a proportion of GNP and expansion of military manpower, also greatly favored the underdeveloped, rather than the developed, world. What is even more distressing is that "gunboat diplomacy" is becoming vastly more commonplace in the third world as it is shunned as valueless by the Western democracies. The examples can be easily recounted.

New influences in a new context, then, must be central to our discussion.

PHILIP KARBER (Vice President of BDM, Inc.; Consultant to the Office of the Secretary of Defense): What we need to point out today—and here I disagree with General Graham—is that in the last few years, granting a trail-off following the Vietnam War, the trend in U.S. defense expenditures is decidedly upwards. There are not two curves crossing someplace out on the horizon; rather there are two curves going up. And in the case of the United States, let's be very specific in overall dollar terms. I have the budget figures in front of me. The fiscal budget 1976 in total obligational authority for the United States was $110.8 billion. The estimate for 1977 is $116.9 billion, an increase of 5 percent. Furthermore, even in the slight reductions that Harold Brown has made in the budget proposed by the Republican Administration, this Administration is proposing an increase this year in real dollar terms of 3.5 percent. So the U.S. trend is up.

I would also raise an issue that we haven't discussed here before—that of nuclear proliferation. I would hope that somehow we might bring the arms race between the United States and the Soviet Union a little bit more under control through negotiation so that we can devote more of our diplomatic and political resources to being concerned about the problem of the future—other countries getting the bomb.

I think in that area it would be in our interest to cooperate with, and to get further agreements with, the Soviet Union, to end now the friction that is clearly occurring between the two countries so that we can look to the important problems of the future, one of them certainly being proliferation.

SENATOR CULVER: If I understand the tenor of the discussion today, it essentially discounts the likelihood of an active nuclear exchange with the Soviet Union. But it seems to me that one of the most likely scenarios one might envision, given nuclear proliferation, is not only the more obvious possibility of introduction of nuclear weapons in war because of the proliferation of "scorpions," but the more likely problem posed by subgovernment action, terrorists, and civil war. Here certain elements of even less stability possess a nuclear capability and wish to employ it in scenarios of terrorism or sabotage or blackmail.

More specifically, given the relative ease of attaining a crude nuclear-weapons capability—a capability with nevertheless devastating intimations—I am thinking more in terms of someone in New York who calls President Carter and indicates he has the bomb and is going to blow up New York if certain demands are not met.

What is the capability of the United States in its current defense posture or intelligence determination to cope and deal with that kind of situation? I would suggest for the sake of our discussion that it may well be a far more realistic threat to our survival and political, economic, and social stability.

Secondly, what actually are the most important components of strategic power? But I think that this more specifically raises questions as to what are the elements over and above the simplistic arithmetic of the military balance, which everyone has also agreed has had limitations in effecting an accurate assessment and evaluation of the balance. What about the larger questions that necessarily should be part and parcel of an appropriate evaluation of the strategic balance as distinguished from the military balance?

Again, the qualities and strength of the economic system that are enjoyed by the major powers, the political confidence in their institutions, the morale and the welfare of their people, and most importantly, the reliance of potential allies on the respective sides are all parts of any assessment of the balance. It has been suggested that the Russians are 8 or 12 feet tall, and what not. But the Soviet Union is the only nation in the world that currently is not only surrounded by forward positions—even tactical and strategic nuclear threats. But it is also the only communist country that is surrounded by hostile communist powers.

In the event of a conventional initiation of war what are the implications of the political reliability or unreliability of allies? How does that impact on the balance and relative military strength? I have thrown out a couple of things, but I think we should really focus on two issues here—one is the larger strategic general balance and its equilibrium (including the elements and factors that should be addressed in such an assessment), and secondly this more likely contingent threat to our security and survival posed by the nuclear capabilities of subnational groups and terrorists.

HERBERT YORK (Professor of Physics, University of California-San Diego; former Director of DDR&E [Doctorate of Defense Research and Engineering] at the Defense Department): I want to comment on the question of terrorism whether by individuals or small groups. I think that nuclear terrorism has been considerably exaggerated—exaggerated on several grounds. The great terrorists of history have all been chiefs of state, not private individuals who have somehow gone and gathered and stolen some plutonium or some other kind of dangerous material at the time. The prime danger is proliferation of nuclear weapons to other states, and their possible use by those states in some uncontrolled way. I also think that the stories about how easy it is to build atomic bombs, while not literally false in the strict technical sense, have always been greatly exaggerated. It is nowhere near as easy as people have suggested. The probability of being caught is much higher than has been allowed for, as is the probability of failure in a dangerous mode. So I don't agree with the implication that I believe I heard here—the possibility that the use of nuclear weapons may be more common to terrorists than to states. It is quite the reverse.

MAJ. GEN. GEORGE KEEGAN, USAF, Ret. (Former Air Force Assistant Chief of Staff for Intelligence): I am glad to report that for the first time in 20 years Dr. York and I have something to agree on. Talk of economic, psychological, subversive, terrorist acts and so forth, I think, have obscured the strategic and tactical questions.

The point I would like to make is this: there is a remarkable body of Soviet evidence that is widely available but seldom read and examined in the free world on questions of military balance, on the questions of total conflict, and how they view and treat surprise. There are not only strategic, tactical, and psychological implications, but also discussions of how these factors are involved in negotiations. That evidence is available. There is a great breadth of translated material on the subject.

With regard to the central character of those materials, it has been my observation that the Soviets have an absolute obsession with strategic power in its broadest dimension whether involving economics, the arts of diplomacy, or trade negotiations. They must come out ahead. This is all a part of the entire dimension of Soviet power with which we must cope. But I think where I enter the picture is at the baseline of all of this—the strategic questions—and there the merits are important.

The Soviets are determined to hold the high ground of strategic superiority because their doctrine, unlike ours, is not focused at avoidance of war. They instead focus on being able to prevail in war and conflict in all of its dimensions—nuclear, conventional, tactical, scientific, and technical.

What you see today is 60 years of crushing their peasantry, bleeding their economy, and disregarding the legitimate needs of society in order that they could advance in this power calculus. Such military advancement is what they seek.

WILLIAM WHITSON (Chief, Foreign Affairs and National Defense Division, Congressional Research Service of the Library of Congress): I would like to address myself to Senator Culver's second question.

We all, I think, have correctly identified almost every factor by which people gain strategic and tactical power. But I believe his second question is really how do we measure the trade-off between military power versus economic and political power—particularly when we have to translate that measurement into budgets, into legislation, into forces and programs, etc. This really relates to John Collins' comment in terms of that kind of calculus. We really have no adequate bureaucratic procedure today. We have taught ourselves to handle military strategy separately. But in search for the trade-off, I am reminded really of the central question: Should we structure our forces in terms of what makes us feel more secure, quite apart from what others may perceive, or should we structure

our forces in order to make the Soviets stay more worried, or the
Chinese? And we get different answers on the questions if we focus
on one part of the question versus the other.

The Chinese—really as late as the end of the Vietnam War,
according to their documents—believed that the United States had,
considering everything, superiority over the Soviets. They didn't
believe this solely because of our material power but instead because
of our flexibility, our ability to move and project power.

Chinese observers worry now about one thing, I think, that has
perhaps not yet been discussed by this group. They worry about our
national will, our consensus, our ability to achieve national agreement. And they call that the fear of Munich, a lack of firmness which
others have raised at this table.

SEN. EDWARD KENNEDY: I believe that it is totally appropriate to
think now of what national security really means in terms of the
American people, as well as to our allies overseas and to those who
depend upon American will and its capacity to respond in strategic
as well as conventional warfare.

I think security means many entirely different things to people
in other parts of the world. In fact, someone just came back from the
World Health Conference this weekend. He stated that there are 80
million children that are born every year. Ten million of them are
being immunized yet many millions of them are dying, despite all
the petitions of those ministers of health and social welfare. Global
instability will certainly come from parents that see the more affluent
and wealthier countries—whether they be the Soviet Union, the United
States, or the countries of Western Europe—able to deal effectively
with the most basic and fundamental issues of human compassion while
they are unable to deal with such needs themselves.

The fact is that over the next 25 years the world population will
double and that anywhere from 75 to 80 percent of those are going to
be brown and yellow and red citizens. What, then, are going to be
the real matters of issue that are going to be before us? As we look
to security requirements in the year 2000, would we not be wise to
begin to anticipate the issues of population and food production and the
various other basic and fundamental questions of social justice?
How are we going to deal effectively with third world countries?

Finally, the issue of basic political stability, as we talk in
terms today about the West and the alliance, will depend on many new
factors, such as European communism, all of which will have the
broadest implications for future U.S. relations with the Soviets and
the Chinese.

Senator Symington then encouraged the participants to present specific policy options for enhancing U. S. security in the remaining decades of the century. Despite the differences in perception indicated by the preceding statements, the later discussions revealed several areas of general agreement: deep concern over a not-too-distant world of many nuclear powers, an acceptance of the likelihood of increased uses of economic coercion, and an appreciation for the inseparability of third-world development and international stability. Questions surrounding the superpower strategic balance are, of course, especially timely. Yet much of the ensuing discussion expanded on the new influences that were noted in the opening statements, such as terrorism, increased defense spending, conflict over scarce resources, third-world despair, population, revolutionary technologies, and so forth. This reflected the concerns of nearly all of the sponsoring senators that a popular preoccupation with the strategic debate tended to obscure these equally complex, and potentially more dangerous, problems that will affect U. S. security for at least the next twenty-five years.

5

SOVIET PERCEPTIONS OF THE MILITARY FACTOR IN THE "CORRELATION OF WORLD FORCES"

Michael J. Deane

INTRODUCTION

When analyzing the relative alignment between communism and capitalism, Soviet spokesmen have, since 1917, contended that the "correlation of world forces" is constantly shifting in favor of communism. Yet explanations of the underlying reasons for this shift have differed considerably over this time span. In view of the Soviet Union's obvious inferiority in concrete areas such as the military or economics, Lenin generally avoided discussion of individual factors in the correlation-of-world-forces calculation, preferring to treat it as a whole or as an assessment of amorphous "class" forces. When Stalin shifted priorities from "world revolution" to "socialism in one country," this was reflected in a change in emphasis in the correlation-of-world-forces assessment so that the impact of conflicts within and between capitalist states, rather than between the two systems, was cited as the reason for the further shift in the world alignment. One major exception to this rule was the importance attached to the defeat of Nazi Germany, which led to the creation of the "socialist community" in Eastern Europe.

Only with Stalin's successors did it again become common to assess the correlation of world forces in terms of a direct capitalist-communist dichotomy. To a significant degree, this derived from the need to explain why intersystemic war was "no longer inevitable," despite the West's military superiority. [1] Thus, in the interpretation of the correlation of world forces, Khrushchev was able to justify a premise which otherwise defied communist ideology. As in the case of Lenin, Khrushchev was deliberately vague in defining the dominant element(s) of the correlation-of-forces assessment, often changing

emphases to meet immediate requirements. Sometimes, as a corollary
of the new stress on "peaceful coexistence" between the two systems,
the economic factor was accented. Frequently, in conjunction with
the revision of the Stalin-Zhdanov "two-camp" thesis, the role of the
newly emerging states, that is, those former colonies which adopted
prosocialist policies, was highlighted.

At other times, especially when seeking to wring concessions
from the West or to deter the West from some course of action (as
during the Suez crisis of 1956, the Berlin crisis of 1958, and the
Cuban missile crisis of 1962), Khrushchev focused upon the military
component in the correlation of world forces. Indeed, Khrushchev
frequently sought to deceive Western leaders with boasts of Soviet
military superiority. On occasion, he asserted that the Soviet Union
possessed "the absolute weapon" so that an intersystemic war would
end "with the destruction of capitalism."[2] Again, during a 1960 visit
to Austria, Khrushchev claimed that the Soviet Union was militarily
the world's most powerful country. [3] In essence, Khrushchev tried
to create uncertainties in the West with regard to the strategic
balance, with the intent that such uncertainties would constrain
Western foreign-policy activity.

To whatever extent this approach was successful, it was offset
in the early 1960s as the United States gained a better satellite
surveillance and U-2 overflight capability. Thus, the "missile gap"
myth that Khrushchev had worked so hard to create soon dissipated
under improved U. S. reconnaissance techniques. It was at this
juncture that Khrushchev made the decision to install strategic
weapons in Cuba as a quick and cheap method of countering U. S.
strategic superiority. Detected before they became operational,
however, the missiles were withdrawn under U. S. pressures. At
the time, Khrushchev threatened to use the missiles and planes in
Cuba against U. S. territory and to employ Soviet submarines against
American ships, but by far the most ominous warning came from
Soviet Deputy Foreign Minister V. V. Kuznetsov, who assured one
U. S. official: "Never will we be caught like this again."[4]

In essence, the correlation-of-world-forces concept began as
an amorphous idea of "class" relations. It proved to be a handy tool
for Lenin, and later Stalin, to justify or oppose certain courses of
action insofar as the assessment was not independently verifiable
through the calculation of any concrete indexes. Under Khrushchev,
correlation of world forces became an instrument not only to formulate Soviet foreign policy, but also to constrain Western freedom of
action. In this respect, Khrushchev found that emphasis on the
economic factor or newly emerging states had some propaganda
appeal, but turning these into direct foreign policy gains vis-à-vis
the West was difficult. Conversely, he believed that, if he could

convince the West of a shift in the correlation of military forces, significant gains might follow. Khrushchev's problem, however, was that his assertions of military superiority were grounded on deception, not fact. Once this deception was revealed, the former constraints on the West disappeared. The prime example of this change in attitude was the determination of the United States during the Cuban missile crisis.

The purpose of this study is to analyze the current Soviet leadership's concept of the correlation of world forces and to assess the role and importance that the leadership attaches to the military factor within the overall concept.

THE CURRENT LEADERSHIP'S VIEW OF THE "CORRELATION OF WORLD FORCES"

In the current Soviet literature, the correlation-of-world-forces concept is defined as the aggregation of all domestic and international indexes and factors which impact on the relative alignment of capitalism and communism. Indeed, Soviet commentators describe the "correlation of world forces" as a multidimensional concept, which encompasses "the correlation of <u>class</u> forces and the struggle of classes both in individual countries and in the international arena, taking into account those <u>real</u> forces—economic, political, moral, and others—which stand behind these classes"[5] (emphasis in original). In fact, the number of factors which may be included in the correlation-of-world-forces assessment is open-ended and limited only by objective circumstances. As one Soviet spokesman has explained, "the mobility, dynamism, and changeability" of the correlation of world forces is a reflection of the "complexity and multitudinous aspects" of the concept wherein "the part played by some factors is growing, that of others is diminishing; they interact and sometimes cancel out one another."[6]

According to their nature, the elements within the correlation of world forces fall into two categories: (1) the material component, which includes the economic and military factors; and (2) the nonmaterial component, which covers the sociopolitical and ideological factors. One major reason for this distinction in Soviet literature is the fact that the material component is capable of a quantifiable calculation on the whole, whereas the nonmaterial component, for the most part, has to be qualitatively evaluated. Quite obviously, qualitative assessments present certain problems for the determination of a foreign policy which is to be "scientifically substantiated." However, Soviet spokesmen are adamant that both components must be weighed because the nonmaterial factors "are inseparably linked with the material factors; it is often difficult to separate one from the other. "[7]

Despite this problem, correlation-of-world-forces assessments are said to serve three functions. First, they provide not only a historical background but also an accurate description of the state of international affairs at any particular moment. Second, since clashes in the international arena are ultimately determined by the correlation of world forces, these assessments provide a long-range historical view of the prospects of world development. Third, and perhaps most importantly, they provide the scientific framework in which critical choices are made from among a wide range of foreign-policy, strategic, and tactical options. [8]

As long-term analyses of historical trends, the correlation-of-world-forces assessments appraise the aggregate of events within an extended "epoch." Thus, while individual successes and failures will affect the correlation of world forces at any given moment, qualitative changes have been few. Indeed, to this point, contemporary Soviet commentators identify only three major stages in the historical development of the correlation of world forces. The first stage began with the Bolshevik Revolution, when the first socialist state emerged as a counterweight to the "imperialist-capitalist states." The second stage started with the defeat of Nazi Germany, the appearance of communist-controlled states in Eastern Europe, and the breakup of the old colonial empires. The third and most recent stage is dated from the period 1969-70 and is closely connected with the "fundamental restructuring" of international relations allegedly occurring as a result of the onset of strategic-nuclear parity between the two super-powers. While the first two represented relative changes in the correlation of world forces during which the Soviet Union made significant gains vis-à-vis the United States, the third change was characterized as an absolute change in the capitalist-communist alignment such that the Soviet Union was no longer inferior to the United States. As it will be shown later, the distinguishing factor here was the public recognition given to the 1969-70 shift by the Western leadership. In this sense, the third shift in the correlation of world forces marks an especially important milestone in the historical development of world communism.

Yet, three caveats must herein be noted. [9] First, the East-West relationship is viewed from the perspective of a "zero-sum" situation. Every loss by the capitalist side is seen as a positive gain from the communist side, and every capitalist achievement is considered a net loss for communism. Therefore, while qualitative changes are said to transpire only infrequently, Soviet analysts are quite sensitive to specific events and indexes, which may have great cumulative effect for the overall trend in historical development.

Second, it is noted that, while the correlation of world forces is a multidimensional concept, the objective international situation precludes the uniform development of all factors. Insofar as the Soviet Union is only one of many actors in international affairs, the Soviets are not always in a position to manipulate the various elements to the fullest extent desired. Consequently, the importance of individual factors will be uneven and may tend to fluctuate over time.

Third, on the subjective level, there is no requirement that all elements of struggle must be actively and equally pursued by the Soviets or their opponents at any given time. Indeed, it is pointed out that states will emphasize those forms and methods which, in their opinion, are most effective in a given situation. While there are no "neutral areas," the degree of competition enjoined in any individual area is dictated by such notions as feasibility, opportunity, and necessity, as well as the staunchness of the opponent to assume the struggle. This also means, therefore, that the importance attached to individual factors in the correlation of world forces will not remain constant. Such importance will change as foreign-policy potentials and tactics change.

As a result, some Soviet spokesmen have discussed the relative importance of the various factors within the correlation of world forces assessment. Some have suggested that the military element is the most significant, others the economic element, while others still stress the interdependence and interaction of all elements. [10] A closer examination, undertaken directly below, of Soviet views on the third historical stage in the correlation will reveal, however, that the leadership accepts the military element as the decisive factor in the fundamental restructuring of the correlation characterizing that stage.

THE SOVIET VIEW OF THE THIRD STAGE IN THE "CORRELATION OF WORLD FORCES": ORIGINS AND IMPACT

In the Soviet world view, the Western capitalist states are, by definition, aggressive, militarist, and the source of all wars. Moreover, it is claimed that they are feverishly making military preparations to attack and destroy the communist camp. (See discussion below on the Soviet view of U. S. military doctrine and strategy.) Lest anyone should mistakenly surmise that the nature of "imperialism" has changed in the era of detente, CPSU General Secretary Leonid Brezhnev set forth the line that "although the possibilities of aggressive imperialist actions are now significantly reduced, its nature remains as before. [11]

However, the Soviets contend that a countervailing trend has been gaining in importance and influence over recent years. It is based on the so-called "realistic forces" or "sober-minded circles" in the West, who have come "to an understanding of the limited role of military force in the contemporary world and the hopelessness of converting military might into a fetish to which economic and domestic political interests are sacrificed."[12] Still, it is pointed out that even this stratum of the bourgeoisie has not ceased to be the "class" and ideological opponent of communism. This stratum is realistic not because it has undergone an essential change in nature, but rather because it was forced by objective external circumstances to adopt a new position.[13] It differs from the "reactionary" stratum only by the fact that it perceives an external constraint on its ability to pursue an aggressive and militarist foreign policy.

While the "reactionary forces of the U.S. military-industrial complex" are never depicted as defeated and powerless, it is claimed that President Nixon's election represented a triumph for the "realistic forces."[14] In essence, it is claimed that the Nixon administration was forced by a new correlation of world forces to dispense with its postwar policy of acting from a position of strength, to acknowledge the Soviet Union as an equal participant in international affairs, to accept peaceful coexistence as the guiding principle of international relations, and to enter into a detente or "relaxation of tensions" with the communist states. Such a change, it has been stressed on numerous occasions, was not the result of U.S. good will or morality, but a realistic assessment of the fact that the Soviet Union had attained strategic-nuclear parity with the United States. Commenting on this point, one Soviet spokesman observed that "recognition of Soviet-U.S. parity in strategic armaments was a special factor behind the realization by Western ruling circles of the new realities of our day and the corresponding correction of their political line.[15] The new situation of military parity "forced U.S. ruling circles to revise their foreign policy and military concepts," declared an authoritative study of Soviet foreign policy.[16] In sum, it is maintained that the new military balance had, and continues to have, "a sobering influence on sensible circles in the capitalist world."[17]

From the Soviet standpoint, an objective proof of real strategic nuclear parity is not the issue at hand. Soviet public sources have never demonstrated an interest in concrete comparisons of the numbers and qualities of the two superpowers' weapons. Indeed, the Soviet leadership has traditionally avoided any public acknowledgment of even the most rudimentary military information either for its own people or for discussion at arms-control and disarmament negotiations.

Proof of the parity situation is drawn from statements by American government officials and academics and other authoritative Western publications. The important factor, then, was the perception and public admission by Western decision makers that strategic nuclear parity had occurred and that this situation was cause for a reexamination and modification of U. S. foreign policy.

Also important was the fact that the military component was the decisive component which forced the U. S. to its new perception of the correlation of world forces. In essence, therefore, despite occasional statements to the contrary, it becomes evident that the Soviet leadership recognizes the overriding significance of the military component for all of the other areas of competition. In other words, Soviet military might, particularly its strategic-nuclear capability, is the foundation for the attainment of success in all other areas of struggle. Such emphasis on strategic-nuclear weapons does not imply that the Soviets have been little concerned with tactical and theater-war fighting capabilities. Indeed, Soviet motorized combat vehicles and artillery—to name but two items—have been significantly improved. It only means that in the correlation-of-world-forces calculation primary concern is attached to strategic nuclear weapons.

Given this general background, it is now necessary to turn attention to the more specific utility attached to military power, as well as Soviet attempts to increase this power as a means to further shift the correlation of world forces.

SOVIET VIEWS ON THE UTILITY OF WAR AND THE ARMED FORCES

Historically, the tendency among U. S. leaders has been to view the use of military force, or the threat of the use of military force, as a means of last resort and then only to restore the status quo. It is employed only when all other avenues have proven inadequate. In such instances, as events following World Wars I and II, the Korean War, and the Vietnam War illustrate, the cessation of hostilities has been cause for the rapid dismantling of wartime capabilities.

The Soviets, on the other hand, have looked upon military might and the threat of military might as an integral part of Soviet foreign policy. As one Soviet observer pointed out:

Unquestionably, military force plays a great role in relations among states. The status and size of the actual armed forces and the military-economic potential of states are factors, which to a significant

degree determine the part played by a state or group
of states in the development of contemporary international processes. [18]

From the Soviet perspective, military power creates certain political
and military advantages which can be, and indeed must be, exploited
to the detriment of the opponent.

On the political side, the Soviet leadership views military
power as a vital instrument. This derives from the fact that
"imperialism normally retreats when faced by a superior force."[19]
It is only the existence of a powerful Soviet military instrument that
"restrains the ardor of the most aggressive imperialist circles and
blocks the path of their aggressive intentions."[20] Indeed, it is
constantly emphasized in Soviet literature that "the gains of the
toilers of the USSR and the other fraternal countries would undoubtedly
have been threatened if the military might of the socialist community,
primarily the Soviet Union, had not protected them from the
aggressive imperialist forces."[21] In other words, despite continuous
assertions of overtaking the West economically, it is the military
component which is accepted as the key element from among the
various elements that can be brought to bear against the West.

Even outside of the direct U.S.-USSR relationship, Soviet
commentators claim that the decisive factor in the postwar success
of "national liberation" movements was the existence of a strong
Soviet military. It is maintained that the Soviet armed forces prevent
the Western states from effectively dealing with procommunist
factions in the Third World.[22]

On the military side, the Soviet leadership rejects the contention that nuclear weapons have made wars inconceivable. Following
the last Nixon-Brezhnev summit, for example, Brezhnev observed
that "it would be completely dangerous if the opinion became firmly
established in public circles that everything is now completely in
order and that the threat of war has become illusory."[23] Thus,
Soviet commentators continuously declare that "the danger of war
continues to be a grim reality of our day."[24] This means that, as
first espoused by Clausewitz and later adopted by Lenin, war
continues to be a weapon and instrument of politics—a fact which
will be nullified only with the demise of capitalism and is in no way
linked with the improvement of weapons. As one Soviet political
officer explained:

The thesis of Marxism-Leninism on war as a continuation
of politics by military means remains true under conditions of radical changes in military affairs. The
attempt of some bourgeois ideologues to prove that

nuclear-missile weapons remove war outside the
framework of politics and that nuclear war is outside the control of politics, has ceased to serve as
a weapon of politics, and will not be its continuation
is incorrect in a theoretical respect and reactionary
in a political respect. [25]

The corollary of the possibility of war, from the Soviet
perspective, is the necessity to develop and maintain a military
capability not merely to repel, but to attain victory over, an enemy.
Commentators frequently invoke Lenin's dictum that "victory is won
by he who has the best equipment, organization, discipline, and the
finest hardware. "[26]
While such statements appear to reflect the dominant line,
they must be balanced with the observation that some dissent has
recently been registered in the Soviet press. For example, several
high-ranking Soviet officials have suggested that a new world war
between the two superpowers "could turn into the destruction of
civilization. "[27] Even Brezhnev has declared that "if the presently
accumulated supply of weapons were launched, mankind could be
completely destroyed. "[28] Indeed, the Director of the Moscow State
Institute of International Relations Under the Ministry of Foreign
Affairs has gone so far as to proclaim that mutual, assured destruction is a fact of life. Accordingly, he observed:

The military-technical revolution has led to the creation
of the most destructive means of war, which surpass by
many times anything that was used in previous wars. A
situation has arisen in which the belligerents can not
only destroy each other but also severely damage the
very conditions of mankind's existence. Nuclear-missile
war can no longer be a rational means of attaining
political aims in international relations. From this
standpoint, war ceases to be a continuation of politics,
as it was defined in his time by Clausewitz. [29]

In sum, since a worldwide nuclear war would destroy civilization, including the superpower combatants, neither can reasonably use
it to achieve political aims. Consequent to this view is the premise
that pursuit of military superiority over the opponent will not provide
any appreciable advantage. The prominent Soviet military analyst,
General Major R. Simonyan, doctor of military science and frequent
commentator on military matters in Krasnaya zvezda, maintained
in June 1977 that "indeed, with the equality of strategic forces and
when both sides possess weapons capable of destroying all life on

earth many times over, neither the addition of new batches of weapons
nor the raising of their destructive force can yield any substantial
military and, still less, political advantage. "[30]

These dissenters may be representative of a certain deviant
segment of the Soviet leadership. However, as many Western observers contend, they may be espousing merely a propaganda line for
Western consumption. The task here is not to judge between these
two possibilities. It is sufficient for present purposes only to note
that, while such viewpoints are not new in the Soviet Union, they are
not characteristic of the prevailing Soviet position. The dominant
(that is, the official) line posits that military power retains both
political and military utility in the nuclear era. It is necessary,
therefore, to examine Soviet attempts to shift the correlation of
military forces in its favor.

SOVIET ATTEMPTS TO SHIFT THE
"CORRELATION OF MILITARY FORCES"

As noted earlier, the Soviets view the correlation of world
forces from the perspective of a zero-sum game. This equally
applies to the correlation of individual elements in the overall
alignment. In concrete terms, this means that the correlation of
military forces is considered to be a dual process, wherein it is
important not only to build up Soviet forces but also to inhibit U.S.-
NATO buildup as much as possible.

The Soviets seek to portray the arms race as Western-inspired,
especially by the U.S. military-industrial complex which derives
"huge profits" from the constant improvement of weapons and the
further development of new systems. Especially dangerous, charged
one Soviet political analyst, is the Pentagon's preparation of "a
broad program for the development of new systems of mass-destruction
weapons. "[31] In this connection, Soviet spokesmen severely condemn
specific U.S. weapons systems—such as the B-1 bomber, the Trident
submarine, the cruise missile, and the neutron bomb—as well as
more esoteric types—binary and nerve gases, lasers, and those utilizing antimatter, genetic, and geophysical properties. [32] The Soviets
argue that unless such weapons and systems are banned the Soviet
Union will be forced to respond to their development by creating
systems which it would otherwise never consider producing.

Indeed, to this end the Soviets have introduced a United Nations
proposal for a world-disarmament conference to reach a ban on
further qualitative improvements leading to "new types and new
systems of weapons of mass destruction. "[33] The rationale for the

proposal was first voiced by Brezhnev, who spoke in mid-1975 on the urgency

> to conclude an agreement on the ban on manufacturing new categories of mass-destruction weapons, and new systems of such weapons. At the level of present-day science and technology there arises a grave danger that an even more terrible weapon will be created. The common sense and conscience of mankind impose the necessity of erecting an insurmountable barrier to the appearance of such a weapon. [34]

Since that time, Soviet publications have consistently maintained that the Soviet Union is fully prepared to conclude such an agreement, but is prevented from doing so only by the intransigence of U. S. "reactionary" forces. In light of past experience in attempting to get basic quantitative data on military manpower and equipment from the Soviets, it is quite obvious that the Soviet proposal for banning new weapons serves nothing but a propaganda function. If the Soviets have refused basic quantitative data, it is unrealistic to expect that they would supply the extensive information on Soviet research and development capabilities to verify any agreement on banning new weapons. In advancing a proposal that has great popular appeal in the abstract, the Soviets are not in the least concerned with simultaneously advancing the specifics which would make an agreement feasible.

Similarly, the Soviets proposed to the U. N. in September 1973 that all Security Council members reduce their military expenditures by 10 percent and use part of the savings to aid the developing countries. Again, a proposal with worthwhile intent in the abstract had no possibility in practice. It was impossible not only because the PRC, a Security Council member, would assuredly have vetoed it, but also because the Soviets absolutely refuse to acknowledge the true level of Soviet military expenditures. In the Soviet budget, defense spending is given as a single, one-line figure of approximately 17 billion rubles or about 23 to 25 billion dollars. [35] Thus, while the proposal may have had some propaganda appeal among Third World elites or Western arms control and disarmament advocates, its real objective was to portray the U. S. as the imperialist leader which prefers the arms race to disarmament and Third World development.

Consistent with this image making is the Soviet depiction of U. S. initiatives in the arms control and disarmament arena. Those proposals that the Soviet Union wants to accept are presented as having been forced on the United States. For example, two Soviet commentators noted:

> Despite obvious reluctance of the Western countries to
> enter into genuine disarmament, the radical change in
> the correlation of forces in the international arena in
> favor of socialism, the transformation of the world
> socialist system into the leading force of the present
> day, and the acknowledgment by the capitalist countries
> of the nuclear parity between the USSR and the U. S. A.
> produced a new atmosphere for negotiations that let the
> problem of disarmament gradually move into the area
> of the possible. [36]

Those proposals that the Soviet Union wants to reject are chastized as U. S. attempts to achieve unilateral advantage. According to the Soviet formulation, there presently exists an "essential balance" between Soviet and American strategic-nuclear capabilities as well as between USSR-Warsaw Pact and U. S. -NATO forces in Central Europe. [37] When the Soviets refused even to consider President Carter's March 1977 proposal to the strategic arms limitation talks (SALT)—which aimed not only at the limitation but the actual reduction of some weapons—they did so on the basis that "the U. S. A. is striving to revise the Vladivostok agreement on strategic arms limitation, to gain for itself a one-sided military advantage, and to undermine the Soviet Union's security. "[38] Likewise, in refusing to give up the numerical imbalance created by past Soviet-Warsaw Pact buildups, Soviet spokesmen have characterized Western proposals for asymmetrical disarmament in Central Europe as an attempt "to change the correlation of forces in Central Europe in favor of the West. "[39]

Complementary with this diplomatic offensive is the Soviet program of military construction, which encompasses "the aggregate of economic, sociopolitical, and specifically military measures and efforts of the state, which are carried out in the interests of preparing and waging wars and in the interests of strengthening its military power. "[40] As a writer explained in Krasnaya zvezda, "V. I. Lenin regarded the defense potential of a state as the organized unity of economic, moral-political, and specifically military potential. "[41]

In the moral-political sphere, the Soviet armed forces have created a parallel political structure, the Main Political Administration (MPA) of the Soviet army and navy, among whose responsibilities are the indoctrination of soldiers in the norms of "communist morality. " Each year Soviet officers and soldiers are required to partake in a system of political training in the form of lectures, independent study, and seminars. Officers undergo 50 hours of indoctrination training annually, about one-half of which is given to seminar lessons. Training of nonofficers is more frequent—as much as a two-hour session twice a week. In addition, the MPA supplements the indoctrination with "socialist competition" and "criticism and self-criticism" campaigns for the purpose of whipping up and checking on the ideological conditioning of troops. The ultimate sanction against defects in this sphere is the taking of political and moral qualities into consideration in the selection, placement, and promotion of soldiers. As the chief of the MPA has noted, "the selection and placement of cadres is a political question, not a technical one."[42]

In the economic sphere, Soviet spokesmen frequently observe that there exists a close connection between Soviet economic and military development because "the economy serves as the foundation of defense might."[43] Accordingly, one Soviet military officer and doctor of economic science stated that "Our defense might directly depends on the utmost growth of the USSR's economic might. This dependence is ever increasing due to the growing interrelationship between war and the economy and the growing demands of the army and navy for material resources."[44] Moreover, Soviet commentators openly acknowledge that the Tenth Five-Year Plan adopted in 1976 will emphasize those areas that are most beneficial for weapons development and, therefore, "will be the foundation of new increases in the Soviet Union's economic and defense might."[45]

While it is not possible to determine what the Soviets will spend on military development in the Tenth Five-Year Plan, there is every reason to believe that the previous trend will continue. In a dollar-comparison of U.S. and Soviet defense programs, the Central Intelligence Agency pointed out that the costs of Soviet defense programs exceeded U.S. authorizations in every year since 1970. In 1974 prices, Soviet programs in 1975 (less pension expenditures) cost 50 percent more than U.S. programs. In terms of constant U.S. prices, which measure growth in real terms, there has been a continuous growth during the period 1965-1975 of about 3 percent per year (as compared to the United States, whose authorizations in constant-dollar terms have declined continuously since 1968 and, since 1973, have fallen below the 1965 level).[46]

In the military sphere proper, Soviet efforts appear to affirm the Kuznetsov "never again" warning of 1962. Since that time, the Soviets have undertaken a military development program that has not only overcome the former U.S. superiority but also created a capability beyond what many Western military experts consider necessary for Soviet defensive purposes. Soviet active-duty manpower is more than double that of the United States and Soviet ground forces alone outnumber all active U.S. forces by about 400,000. Since 1962,

the United States has deployed only four new ICBM systems, while
the Soviets have deployed ten. Subsequent to the latest U.S. deployment in 1970, the Soviets have introduced five new systems. Similarly,
the U.S. has deployed only three new submarine-launched ballistic
missile (SLBM) systems since 1962 and only one after 1964, whereas
the Soviets have deployed four, of which three were introduced later
than 1964. Moreover, Secretary of Defense Harold Brown revealed
in September 1977 that "the Soviets have four new ICBMs under
development, they are continuing work on the SS-16, their mobile
ICBM, and they are modifying four other missiles."[47]

Quite obviously, present limitations do not allow for a total
assessment of Soviet military programs, but the point to be stressed
here is that such programs underscore the complete Soviet rejection
of any concept to limit plans for military development. In this respect,
Soviet military thinking is devoid of any concept akin to the U.S.
idea of "sufficiency" in military construction. In their formulation,
it is asserted that every achievement "must be considered only as the
next step in turn for the further raising of the armed forces' combat
might."[48] This is particularly true insofar as the East-West military
competition has switched "from the plane of a numerical buildup of
'big battalions' into the plan of qualitatively improving new
hardware."[49]

According to the late Marshal of the Soviet Union, I.I.
Yakubovskiy, there are two basic trends in Soviet weapons development: (1) the development of current arms and systems, and (2)
the development and creation of fundamentally new systems.[50] For
many years, greater practical emphasis was placed on a steady
improvement in current weapons instead of waiting for qualitative
improvements that require some time lag for design and production.
More recently, Soviet open literature has begun to stress the need for
developing fundamentally new systems. As one Soviet expert explained:

> Inasmuch as there are no limits to understanding natural
> laws, so there can be no limits to the application of these
> laws in technical designs. From this point of view, the
> most terrible weapon cannot be called absolute since in
> its stead can come a still more powerful one based on
> the newest scientific-technical achievements.[51]

Given this view, the Soviets maintain that the quest for scientific
and technical superiority is mandated not only for the contemporary
advantages it may give vis-à-vis a potential opponent, but also because
superiority, once attained, is not necessarily permanent. With this
in mind, Marshal A. A. Grechko wrote in The Armed Forces of the
Soviet State that Soviet military-technical policy must orient research

not only toward the solution of "current" problems, but also toward "the solution of various long-term problems whose results might find wide application in military affairs in the future," especially "basic research directed toward the discovery of yet unknown characteristics of matter, phenomena, and laws of nature, and the development of new methods of studying and utilizing them for strengthening the state's defense capability."[52]

SOVIET VIEW OF THE IMPACT OF THE "CORRELATION OF MILITARY FORCES" ON U. S. MILITARY DOCTRINE AND STRATEGY

In the Soviet view, foreign policy is not formulated in the abstract. It is determined by the interests and goals of the dominant class. Since Soviet foreign policy supposedly reflects the interests and goals of the "workers and toilers," it is claimed to be "peace loving." It follows that the military doctrine and strategy selected to implement this policy would be peace loving and defensive. Conversely, since U. S. foreign policy is allegedly a manifestation of the interests and goals of "exploiters and oppressors," it is defined as "imperialist." Thus, the military doctrine and strategy of the United States is "imperialist" and aggressive. Although specific elements of military doctrine and strategy may change over time, their nature is constant. Hence, the Soviet Union will always be the "defender" and the U. S. will always be the "aggressor." In the words of one Soviet analyst:

> V. I. Lenin taught that the real nature of war is
> determined not by who attacked first, on whose terri-
> tory war is being conducted, or whether the fighting is
> offensive or defensive. It is important to consider "what
> class nature the war bears, for what reasons the war
> has broken out, what class is waging it, and what
> historic and historical-economic conditions provoked
> it.[53]

Consequently, the nature of U. S. doctrine and strategy remains constant, but its content has undergone significant change.

The Soviets divide post-World War II U. S. military doctrine and strategy into three stages, with changes occurring "roughly every decade in connection with radical shifts in the correlation of forces in the world and the development of the means of armed struggle."[54] The first period, from 1945-1960, was based upon the policy of containment, which gave rise to the strategy of "massive retaliation." According to the Soviets, massive retaliation "envisioned the preparation and the conduct of a 'preventive' nuclear war, which was considered in imperialist strategy as a unilateral act of nuclear assault, against the countries of the socialist community. "[55] However, by the end of the 1950s the United States was "forced" to reevaluate its position because "in all decisive areas of military affairs the Soviet Union was not behind the U.S.A. and in a number of areas passed ahead of it. "[56]

This reassessment led to the development of a new strategy, namely, flexible response, which dominated between 1961 and 1971. While still espousing to deal "from a position of strength," the new strategy considered a growing "balance" of U.S. and Soviet strategic capabilities, say Soviet commentators. Now, nuclear war would not be unilateral, but a mutual exchange of nuclear strikes. Further refinements of flexible response included the concepts of escalation and two-and-a-half wars, i.e. being prepared to fight at the same time major conflicts in the NATO area and the Pacific and a minor campaign elsewhere.

At the beginning of the 1970s, strategic-nuclear parity again "forced" the United States to reevaluate its military strategy. This stage began with the enunciation of the "realistic deterrence" strategy, relying on the concepts of strategic sufficiency, one-and-a-half wars, strategic mobility, and limited strategic war. While acknowledging that U.S. military power continues to grow, the Soviets stress that the devolution of U.S. strategy reflects a decreasing utility of this power as a consequence of the "objective changes in the correlation of forces in favor of socialism"[57]—which in this case means the growth of Soviet military might.

In essence, therefore, the trend in U.S. doctrine and strategy is significant not only for what it reveals concerning U.S. war-fighting concepts, but also for its implications for the correlation of military forces in particular and the correlation of world forces in general. From the Soviet perspective, the reexamination and subsequent modification of U.S. military doctrine and strategy roughly every decade transpired because of the shifting correlation of world forces. Yet, beyond this, the changes in U.S. military doctrine and strategy are, in a sense, a measure of the shift in the correlation of world forces and a confirmation of the utility of Soviet military development.

Within this context, however, it is necessary to note that Soviet analysts do find certain elements of the current U.S. military strategy to be quite unsettling. Given the overall trend that U.S. military might was being effectively constrained, the Soviets reacted quite vehemently to the U.S. announcement of new positions on the use of limited nuclear war and selective targeting. Whereas previously American strategy made an attack on Soviet territory very unlikely,

the new concepts heightened the possibility that Soviet territory
would now be more vulnerable to attack if conflict should occur.
Soviet analysts overlooked the proposition that the U. S. first use of
nuclear weapons against selected targets would be a response to
Soviet tactical, conventional gains in Central Europe. They equated
first use with preemption and charged the United States was seeking
to blur the distinction between nuclear and conventional warfare.

In sum, therefore, the credibility of Soviet nuclear deterrence
has been somewhat eroded insofar as the United States appears to no
longer accept the Soviet contention that an attack on the USSR's
territory will in all likelihood escalate to total nuclear war. Since
nuclear parity "forced" the United States to give up acting from a
position of strength and to accept peaceful coexistence, it is dis-
concerting in that a rejection of U. S. unilateral military constraint
may lead to the U. S. rejection of political constraint. Indeed, since
it is not the good will or rationality of the West which restrains it,
but rather Soviet military power, any policy which alleviates U. S.
restraint is—in a zero-sum calculation—a policy which inhibits Soviet
freedom of action.

CONCLUDING REMARKS

In summary, contemporary Soviet spokesmen maintain that
the overall trend in the correlation of world forces is constantly shifting in favor of communism. According to the Soviet definition, "correlation of world forces" is an aggregate of all factors and indexes
that affect the relative alignment between the two opposing systems.
In actual fact, the Soviet leadership's calculation of the correlation
of world forces relies heavily upon an assessment of the military
component. This is the fundamental element not only because Soviet
military strength is the single index that allows the Soviet Union to
claim superpower status but also because Western political decision
makers have officially acknowledged the Soviet's attainment of
strategic-nuclear parity, and, therewith, have modified their
approaches to foreign policy.

Given the importance of the military factor, the Soviets have
utilized several methods to shift the correlation of military forces
further in their favor. On the one hand, they have tried diplomatic
and propagandistic moves with the aim of halting, or at least retarding,
Western military construction. They seek to reinforce that sector of
Western opinion which contends that war in a nuclear era is unthink-
able and, therefore, not really possible. At the same time, the Soviet
leadership seeks to instill in its own people the conviction that war
is possible and that, as a consequence, great spiritual and material

sacrifices must be made in order to create a war-fighting and war-winning capability.

In an attempt to test the sincerity of Soviet claims to a radical shift in the correlation of world forces due to the achievement of strategic-nuclear parity in 1969-70, the question frequently arises: What have the Soviets done since 1969-70 that they would not have done under previous conditions? Such a question implies the expectation that the Soviets will use their new position to further communist expansionist aims.. One line of reasoning might extrapolate from Soviet risk taking of earlier and more vulnerable periods to suggest that the stronger the Soviets become militarily, the more risks they will undertake.

Such an argument may have some validity as exemplified by Soviet-Cuban involvement in the Angolan war or by Soviet threats and mobilization during the Arab-Israeli war of 1973. However, it is too simplistic to measure the Soviet perception of the shifting correlation of world forces only in terms of overt Soviet military acts. Because of their past military inferiority, the Soviets have, by force of circumstances, developed a concept of power that is multidimensional. While such power depends on military might, it is often manifested through economic influence, ideological persuasion, and political prestige. Thus, from the Soviet viewpoint, the current correlation of world forces frees the Soviet Union to pursue many arenas of competition with the West, while its level of military development gives the assurance that the United States will not respond with a real threat to Soviet survival.

Moreover, there is no imperative that the Soviet Union must "do something" with the new correlation of world forces. The Soviets may find it quite sufficient that (1) the United States has acknowledged the USSR as one of the two major actors on the international scene without whose agreement the settlement of conflict situations, as in the Middle East, would be impossible and (2) the United States has in the past three decades modified not only its foreign policy but also its military doctrine and strategy in consideration of increasing Soviet power. In this sense, the Soviets have gained without risk to the Soviet Union. Consequently, Soviet military might has developed into real power infofar as it has achieved influence over Western behavior without having actually resorted to force or the threat of force.

In conclusion, the importance of the military factor in the "correlation of world forces" derives as much from the perception (that is, Western evaluation) of Soviet strength as it does from the weapons of the Soviet armed forces.

NOTES

1. N. S. Khrushchev, "Accountability Report of the Central Committee of the Communist Party of the Soviet Union to the Twentieth Party Congress," The Twentieth Congress of the Communist Party of the Soviet Union: Stenographic Report, vol. 1 (Moscow: Politizdat, 1956), pp. 37-38.

2. "Conversation of N. S. Khrushchev with Editor-in-Chief W. R. Hearst," Pravda, November 29, 1957, and "Speech of Comrade N. S. Khrushchev at the Ninth All-German Workers' Conference in Leipzig, March 7, 1959," Pravda, March 27, 1959.

3. "We Are Striving for a Better Life and for the Most Beautiful Life on Earth," Pravda, July 8, 1960.

4. Quoted in John Newhouse, Cold Dawn: The Story of SALT (New York: Holt, Rinehart and Winston, 1973), p. 68.

5. Sh. Sanakoyev, "The Problem of the Correlation of Forces in the Contemporary World," Mezhdunarodnaya zhizn' 10 (October 1974): 42.

6. D. Tomashevsky, Lenin's Ideas and Modern International Relations (Moscow: Progress Publishers, 1974), pp. 83-84.

7. Sanakoyev, op. cit. , p. 46.

8. See, for example, G. Shakhnazarov, "New Factors in Politics at the Present Stage," Social Sciences (Moscow) 8, no. 1 (1977): 39; and V. V. Zagladin, ed. , The World Communist Movement. Outline of Strategy and Tactics (Moscow: Progress Publishers, 1973), pp. 36, 41.

9. On the caveats, see Boris Ponomarev, "The Role of Socialism in Contemporary World Development," Problemy mira i sotsializma 1 (January 1975): 11; Tomashevsky, op. cit. , p. 102; and V. M. Kulish, Military Force and International Relations (Moscow: International Relations Publishers, 1972), p. 217.

10. See, for example, G. Shakhnazarov, "Victory—Correlation of Forces—Peaceful Coexistence," Novoye vremya 19 (May 1976): 6; D. Proekter, "Socialism and International Security," Kommunist 7 (May 1977): 115; I. Kuz'minov, "The Deepening of the General Crisis of Capitalism," International Affairs, 7 (July 1976): 5; and S. Tyushkevich, "The Correlation of Forces in the World and Factors of War Prevention," Kommunist Vooruzhenykh Sil 10 (May 1974): 12.

11. L. I. Brezhnev, "Report of the CPSU Central Committee and the Immediate Tasks of the Party in the Area of Domestic and Foreign Policy," The Twenty-fifth Congress of the Communist Party of the Soviet Union. Stenographic Report, vol. 1 (Moscow: Politizdat, 1976), p. 47.

12. V. V. Zhurkin, "Approach to Negotiations," in Yu. P. Davydov, V. V. Zhurkin, and V. S. Rudnev, eds., Doktrina Niksona (Moscow: Nauka Publishers, 1972), p. 44.

13. V. F. Petrovskiy, "On Contemporary U. S. Foreign Policy Concepts," U. S. A. : Economics, Politics, Ideology 8 (August 1977): 20.

14. See, for example, L. M. Gromov and R. A. Faramazyan, Voyennaya ekonomika sovremennogo kapitalizma (Moscow: Voyenizdat, 1975), passim; and B. D. Pyadyshev, The Military-Industrial Complex of the U. S. A. (Moscow: Progress Publishers, 1977), passim.

15. D. Tomashevsky, "How the West is Reacting to Détente," International Affairs (Moscow) 11 (November 1976): 38.

16. A. A. Gromyko and B. N. Ponomarev, Istoriya vneshney politiki SSSR, vol. 1 (Moscow: Nauka Publishers, 1976), p. 588-89.

17. "Twenty-fifth Party Congress on the Strengthening of the Country's Defense Potential and the Soviet Armed Forces' Combat Might. Tasks of the Personnel for Further Raising the Combat Readiness of Units and Ships," Kommunist Vooruzhennykh Sil 9 (May 1976); 74.

18. G. F. Vorontsov, Voyennyye koalitsii i kolitsionnyye voyny (Moscow: Voyenizdat, 1976), p. 310.

19. Tomashevsky, Lenin's Ideas and Modern International Relations (Moscow: Progress Publishers, 1974), p. 97.

20. General-Major S. Tyushkevich, "Fruits of Creative Labor Under a Reliable Protection," Kommunist Vooruzhennykh Sil 11 (June 1976): 16.

21. Colonel I. Forofonov, "How to Conduct Lessons With Young Soldiers and Sailors," Kommunist Vooruzhennykh Sil 5 (March 1974): 71.

22. Colonel A. Timorin, "Leninist Doctrine on Defense of the Socialist Homeland and Modern Times," ibid. 22 (November 1973): 14. See also V. V. Zagladin, "Changes in the World and the Communist Movement," Rabochiy klass i sovremennyy mir 5 (September-October 1975): 5.

23. L. I. Brezhnev, "Socialist Poland—Thirty Years," Leninskim kursom, vol. 5 (Moscow: Politizdat, 1976), p. 118.

24. Colonel V. Khalipov, "The Aggressive Nature of Contemporary Imperialism," Kommunist Vooruzhennykh Sil 1 (January 1976): 70. See also Lieutenant-Colonel A. Kor'kov, "USSR Armed Forces in the Postwar Period," ibid. 13 (July 1976): 75.

25. S. Tyushkevich, "Development of the Teaching on War and the Army from the Experience of the Great Fatherland War," Kommunist Vooruzhennykh Sil 22 (November 1975): 11. See also V. M. Bondarenko, Sovremennaya nauka i razvitiye voyennogo dela

(voyenno-sotsiologicheskiye aspekty problemy) (Moscow: Voyenizdat, 1976), pp. 130-32.

26. See, for example, B. S. Tel'pukhovskiy, "The Activity of the CPSU for Strengthening USSR Defense in the Years of the Socialist Reconstruction of the National Economy," Voprosy istorii KPSS 8 (August 1976): 87; and General Major M. Cherednichenko, "Scientific-Technical Progress and Some Problems of Military Science," Kommunist Vooruzhennykh Sil 13 (July 1976): 9.

27. D. Proekter, "Socialism and International Security," Kommunist 7 (May 1977): 109. See also D. M. Gvishiani, Deputy Chairman of the USSR State Committee for Science and Technology (and Kosygin's son-in-law), at the round-table discussion "Science and Global Problems of the Present Day," Voprosy filosofii 10 (October 1974): 51.

28. L. I. Brezhnev, "Meeting of Soviet-Rumanian Friendship," Pravda, November 25, 1976.

29. N. I. Lebedev, "Great October and the CPSU Struggle for Disarmament to the Contemporary Stage," Novaya i noveyshaya istoriya 2 (March-April 1977): 9.

30. General-Major R. Simonyan, "On the Risk of Confrontation," Pravda, June 14, 1977.

31. A. Alekseyev, "Disarmament: Urgent Problems," Pravda, May 21, 1976.

32. See, for example, A. Yefremov, "The Neutron Bomb: Myths and Reality," Krasnaya zvezda, August 14, 1977; S. Novoselov, "Imperialism Without a Mask: Why Does the Pentagon Need Cruise Missiles?" Voyennyye znaniye 1 (January 1977): 44-45; A. G. Arbatov, "'Trident'—A Discussion About the Strategic Program," U. S. A.: Economics, Politics, Ideology 3 (March 1977): 26-36; and General-Lieutenant M. A. Mil'shteyn and Colonel L. S. Semeyko, "The U. S. A. and the Question of New Types of Mass Destruction Weapons," ibid. 5 (May 1976): 25-35.

33. See "Address of A. A. Gromyko," Pravda, September 24, 1975.

34. L. I. Brezhnev, "In the Name of Peace and the Happiness of the Soviet People," ibid., June 14, 1975.

35. Western estimates of Soviet defense spending are much higher. For example, the CIA estimated Soviet expenditures in 1976 at 1970 prices to be about 52 to 57 billion rubles or about 11 to 12 percent of the Soviet GNP. U. S. Congress, Joint Economic Committee, Subcommittee on Priorities and Economy in Government, Allocation of Resources in the Soviet Union and China—1977, Part 1, Hearings in Executive Session, June 23, 1977 (Washington, U. S. Government Printing Office, 1977), pp. 7-8. It must be noted in passing that this figure is considered by many Western observers to be on the low side.

See the discussion in The Military Balance (London: The International Institute for Strategic Studies, 1976), pp. 109-10.

36. N. Ponomarev, and V. Zhuravlev, "The Twenty-fifth CPSU Congress and the USSR Struggle for the Limitation of the Arms Race and Disarmament," Voyenno-istoricheskiy zhurnal 5 (May 1977): 5.

37. D. Proekter, "Dangers, Real and Imaginary," Pravda, January.8, 1977; S. Astakhov, "New Round of Talks," Sotsialicheskaya industriya, September 30, 1977.

38. Vice-Admiral A. Sorokin, "Remarkable Exploit of the Soviet People in the Great Patriotic War," Partiynaya zhizn' 9 (May 1977): 17.

39. V. V. Viktorov and A. V. Staleshnikov, "The Vienna Negotiations: Two-and-a-Half Years Later," U.S.A.: Economics, Politics, Ideology 4 (April 1976), p. 28.

40. Zhilin, Marksistsko-leninskaya metodologiya voyennoy istorii (Moscow: Nauka, 1976), p. 303.

41. Colonel (Reserves) Yu. Korablev, doctor of historical sciences, "Leninist Science Will Prevail," Krasnaya zvezda, September 29, 1977.

42. General of the Army A. A. Yepishev, Mogucheye oruzhiye partii (Moscow: Voyenizdat, 1973), p. 81.

43. Colonel S. Bartenev, "Economic Competition: Conditions, Indicators, Perspectives," Kommunist Vooruzhennykh Sil 2 (January 1976): 24.

44. Colonel Yu. Vlas'yevich, "A Decisive Part of the Struggle for Communism," ibid. 20 (October 1976): 12.

45. "The Sacred Duty and Honorable Obligation of a USSR Citizen," ibid. 16 (August 1976): 74. See also "The Twenty-fifth CPSU Congress and Strengthening the Country's Defense Potential," Voyenno-isotricheskiy zhurnal 10 (October 1976): 6.

46. U.S. Central Intelligence Agency, A Dollar Comparison of Soviet and U.S. Defense Activities, 1965-1975, SR 76-10053 (Washington: CIA, February 1976), p. 3.

47. New York Times, September 16, 1977.

48. "Twenty-fifth Party Congress on Strengthening the Country's Defense Potential and the Soviet Armed Forces' Combat Might," op. cit., p. 80.

49. V. Kortunov, "Arms Race Policy Historically Doomed," International Affairs 10 (October 1976): 5. See also General-Major R. Simonyan, "The Concept of 'Strategic Sufficiency,'" Krasnaya zvezda, August 24, 1976.

50. Marshal of the Soviet Union I. I. Yakubovskiy, "Twenty-fifth CPSU Congress and the Strengthening of the Combat Cooperation

of the Armies of the Warsaw Pact Countries," <u>Voyenno-istoricheskiy zhurnal</u> 8 (August 1976): 8.

    51. Colonel V. Bondarenko, "Soviet Science and Strengthening the Country's Defense," <u>Kommunist Vooruzhennykh Sil</u> 18 (September 1974): 27.

    52. A. A. Grechko, <u>Armed Forces of the Soviet State</u> (Moscow: Military Publishing House, 1975), p. 193.

    53. Colonel V. Izmaylov, "Character and Features of Modern War," <u>Kommunist Vooruzhennykh Sil</u> 6 (March 1975): 68.

    54. Simonyan, "The Concept of 'Strategic Sufficiency,'" op. cit.

    55. Colonel N. Nikitin, "Evolution of U. S. Military Doctrine and Strategic Concepts After World War II," <u>Voyenno-istoricheskiy zhurnal</u> 4 (April 1977): 65.

    56. Vorontsov, <u>Voyennyye koalitsii</u>, op. cit., p. 194.

    57. General Major D. Volkognov, "The Ideological Struggle Under Conditions of the Relaxation of Tensions," <u>Kommunist Vooruzhennykh Sil</u> 3 (February 1977): 17; and G. A. Arbatov at a session of the foreign policy section of the Scientific Council on U. S. Economic, Political, and Ideological Problems, "On Some New Tendencies in the Development of American Military-Strategic Concepts," <u>U. S. A. : Economics, Politics, Ideology</u> 4 (April 1976): 127.

6

THE SUPERPOWER BALANCE, MILITARY POLICY, AND PUBLIC OPNION IN THE UNITED KINGDOM, FRANCE AND THE FEDERAL REPUBLIC OF GERMANY

Robert B. Mahoney, Jr.

INTRODUCTION

This chapter examines the views of British, French, and West German publics concerning national security issues and East-West relations. Its goal is to identify some of the roles which these views have played in the system of postwar East-West competition. Unlike many analyses of public opinion, which emphasize the latest poll results, this study focuses on the analysis of trends in public opinion, since these trends can provide us with a better understanding of the longer-term process of East-West competition. Polls commissioned by the United States Information Agency are used as the principal data source.

The study is divided into three sections. The first presents some of the reasons why we would expect public opinion to have an impact on (and to be influenced by) defense policies and East-West relations and explicates some of the analytical problems which are involved in the analysis of public opinion and its relationships with other factors. The second section traces out some of the broad contours of Western European public opinion. The final section presents an exploratory analysis of the position of Western European public opinion within the

The views expressed in this paper are those of the author and should not be interpreted as representing the policies of Consolidated Analysis Corp., Inc., the Center for Naval Analyses, or any other organization. The author is grateful to Dr. Leo Crespi of the United States Information Agency for his assistance in obtaining some of the data used in this paper.

broader structure of East-West competition and of the relationship
between public opinion and the military balance.

PUBLIC OPINION, THE MILITARY BALANCE,
AND EAST-WEST COMPETITION

The Relevance of Western European Public Opinion

     Public opinion in Western European nations can be related to
defense policy in two ways: as an influence (or constraint) upon the
actions taken by leaders and as an object or target for military and
foreign policies.

Public Opinion as an Influence

     The nations examined here are parliamentary democracies.
Even in open polities such as these, simple electoral mandates—in
which the policy preferences of citizens are directly translated into
government actions—are unlikely to exist. Two factors can account
for the absence of simple mandates. The first is that in the course of
making electoral decisions citizens can consider a wide variety of
domestic and foreign issues which are of varying salience to them. A
vote for candidate X may or may not be a vote for her or his defense
policies; other concerns might be more salient for the bulk of the
electorate. A second factor standing in the way of clear mandates is
the unpredictability of the future. Surprises can occur (for example,
the 1973 oil embargo). The key defense issues at any point may be
matters which were not envisioned at the time of the most recent
election.
     Even in the absence of simple mandates, however, more com-
plex relationships between public opinion and national security policies
are possible and, in some cases, even probable. Elections do allow
voters to make retrospective evaluations of candidates. As a consequence, in many cases candidates will probably attempt to adjust their
policy stances (on national defense as well as other issues) to match
the perceived preferences of the voters, although the dynamics of
this process in the fields of defense and foreign affairs are not well
understood. At the same time, of course, candidates are also likely
to attempt to be leaders by persuading voters to accept their own set of
of policy preferences. The dialectic between these two processes can
result, over time, in a rough general congruence between the
distribution of preferences among the electorate and the policies
advocated by elected officials, even in the absence of a detailed one-

to-one correspondence between the two. Hence, public views on defense issues are likely to have some reflection in policy.

On a more basic level, publics and leaders are constantly involved in the definition of the issues which are of policy concern (for example, what is the standing of human-rights considerations on a nation's foreign policy agenda?). Within any open political order a continuing, often tacit, dialogue takes place in which the nature of the issues (what is the menu?) as well as the positions which nations should take on the issues (what should we order?) are defined and redefined. The relative standings of defense concerns on national policy agendas are likely to be affected by this process, as are the longer-term political career-prospects of candidate leaders.

To the extent that leaders define the universe of relevant issues in the same ways as publics and take positions on the issues that are reasonably consistent with popular opinion, public opinion becomes an important type of resource which leaders can draw upon, leading to policies with greater "resolve". To the extent that incongruencies exist between the leaders and the led, the force of policy actions is likely to be lessened.

Public Opinion as an Object of Policy

Public and elite opinions are identified as important targets for foreign and military policy actions in Soviet and American writings on defense issues. For example, Annual Defense Department Reports by Secretaries of Defense Schlesinger (1975) and Rumsfeld (1976) have expressed concern with such psychological factors as: the need to maintain a rough equivalence between Soviet and American strategic forces to insure that major asymmetries do not develop—thereby avoiding the possibility that misperceptions about the balance might lead to pressures, crises, and confrontations; the requirement that U. S. planners be concerned with the confidence of Western European allies in their ability to resist direct or indirect challenges from the USSR; and the need to consider the peacetime psychological impact of military forces, such as the employment of naval forces to achieve diplomatic influence.

An organizational reflection of these interests has been the creation of the office of the Director of Net Assessment within the Office of the Secretary of Defense. One of the concerns of this office has been the assessment of the psychological impact of Soviet and American forces.

Parallel concern can be found in Soviet writings. Georgi Arbatov, the Director of the Institute of the United States of America and Canada, has emphasized the importance of public opinion in

considerations of interbloc relations. Arbatov argues that tactics
aimed at influencing public opinion are one of the central elements
of modern diplomacy. [1] In his consideration of the role of psychological factors in the "correlations of forces" (or balance of power between
the blocs), Tomashevsky discusses the importance of subjective
factors such as public opinion in terms which are not far removed
from those found in U. S. considerations of net assessment questions:

> The complexity of the category of the balance of power
> and its components is apparent also in the peculiar range
> of objective and subjective factors. For example, the
> subjective factor—evaluation by participants in inter-
> national relations of the relative strength of one
> another and of the general balance of power—may
> sometimes play the role of an element of the objective
> situation. Irrespective of whether such an evaluation is
> correct or not, it may engender certain actions and
> bring about consequences of an altogether objective
> nature, and a change in the objective balance of power.
> In this connection, the role of information (and
> misinformation) is growing in world politics. [2]

Soviet interest in the impact which their politics have upon
public opinion in foreign nations is also reflected in the attention
which recent Soviet foreign-policy writings pay to the results of
Western survey research. [3] There is also reason to believe that the
Soviets are highly concerned with the ramifications that their foreign
policy actions might have upon public opinion within the USSR,
particularly insofar as it might influence the Soviet public's support
of the regime. [4]

Finally, as is the case in the U. S. , this concern with the
importance of public opinion in interstate relations has had organizational manifestations. For example, a recent assessment of the
Soviet Institute of the U. S. A. and Canada notes that it is concerned
with the analysis of American policies, opinions, and attitudes.[5]

Analytical Problems

The analytical problems that need to be considered stem from
two interrelated factors: the nature of the data and the limited amount
of previous research dealing with trends in public opinion and/or with
the relationship between these trends and other factors of
interest.

Data Limitations

The most obvious problems encountered in the analysis of trends in public opinion derive from the analyst's dependence on previous polling efforts. The "right" questions (in the analyst's eyes) may or may not have been asked in the past. A sufficient number of data points for trend analysis may not exist. There may be a sufficient number of item repetitions for trend analysis, but with significant discontinuities in the time series. The values taken by individual observations in the time series may be highly dependent on the precise point at which the item was asked (for example, imagine 1962 polls dealing with Western views of the USSR taken before, during, and after the missile crisis). Attempts to merge similarly worded items can encounter serious problems of item comparability. For the most part, there are no clear-cut solutions to these problems. This study responds to this type of problem by relying on polls commissioned by a single source, which reduces comparability problems. Given this research decision, there is no solution for the problem of gaps in the time series other than to recognize their existence and to consider what implications they have for the substantive conclusions of the analysis.

The data also present some less immediately obvious problems. Most of the available poll items ask respondents to give their views concerning a state of affairs—their attitude or opinion concerning an object (for example, "who is ahead in the military balance")—rather than their opinions concerning policy actions or behaviors ("given the state of military balance, what should our nation do about it?"). This is an important problem for two reasons. The first is that policy preferences are by no means automatically determined by state-of-the-world assessments (the Humean "is"/"ought" dichotomy has its applications in the field of survey research as well as in epistemology). For considerations of defense policy, it is policy questions (what should be done?) that are of the greatest interest, but these are the items which are not, by and large, available. The second problem is that the correlation between an attitude towards an object and subsequent behavior is likely to be weaker than an attitude towards a behavior and subsequent performance of the behavior. [6]

Once again, no true solution is available. The most that can be done is to postulate a plausible linkage or relationship between public opinion and presumed policy preferences (for example, spend more when the balance is perceived to be going against the United States) and to empirically determine if the hypothesized relationship holds true.

A second, subtle, limitation of the data is that public opinion polls do not, by and large, deal with basic political-cultural factors and perceptions. Questions may deal with respondents' views of the Soviet Union and are far less likely to deal with the network of perceptions in which these views operate (for example, is the Soviet Union viewed as an aggressive or as a conservative state?). Once again this is a type of limitation which cannot be surmounted, given available data.

The final problem in this category has to do with the impact of previous world views and policy agendas on the content of questions. The policy agenda which is reflected in a set of survey results may or may not correspond to the policy agenda of an analyst working at a later date; some perceptions of what are "major issues" have changed. Once again, given a decision to rely upon survey data, the only response that can be made to this problem is to recognize it and to be alert for its possible impact on the analysis.

Limitations Due to the Limits of Previous Research

While there have been many studies of public opinion concerning foreign affairs and defense issues, most have focused on the analysis of opinion per se over the short term (usually the most recent poll results). Relatively little work has been done on the analysis of trends and/or the relationship between public opinion and other facets of the international system. Moreover, while some very good theoretical work has been done on the dynamics of the way in which public opinion is interrelated with policy (for example, the two-steps and attentive public models), relatively little empirical work has been done which traces the actual operations of these processes.

As a result of these characteristics of previous research, only relatively weak theoretical "priors" are available to guide this analysis. The absence of strong research priors has serious implications for the employment of regression analysis in the last section of the study, since it results in relatively weak specifications for equations. These relatively weak specifications, in turn, have consequences for the selection of the regression model to be employed in the analysis, for the responses which are made to the problems of multicollinearity and autocorrelation, and for the way in which regression equations are reported and interpreted. *

----

*Standard econometrics texts tend to deal with two classes of problems: (1) situations where strong specifications (based on strong theoretical priors) exist and where attention focuses on regression parameters; and (2) situations where almost no priors exist and where

Ordinary least-squares regression will be employed in the analysis. While OLS cannot capture interactive causality of the sort that is most likely present in the system under consideration, it is fairly robust and relatively well understood. More sophisticated alternative approaches which can capture interactive causal relations require strong specifications of the sort that simply cannot be provided, given the priors which are available.

The regression analysis will focus on the examination of common patterns across indicators (for example, common trends in public opinion and defense expenditures). In this analysis, the pattern-matching components of OLS regression will be emphasized (explanation of variance and the fit between actual and predicted values). Relatively little emphasis will be given to regression coefficients (b's and B's), since these have less importance in the absence of fairly strong specifications. These coefficients will be used, however, to "drive" the residual analyses. *

In the analysis, the existence of multicollinearity and auto-correlation will be noted where appropriate. Because of the relatively weak priors involved, it will not be possible to determine the true causes of these "problems" (for example, how to apportion variance among predictors or whether autocorrelation is due to the omission of one or more explanatory variables, to the mis-specification of the mathematical form of relationship, or to some truly serially dependent process). As a consequence, no response will be made to the presence of either factor.

---

attention focuses almost exclusively on prediction. Many political science problems fall into an intermediate zone, where some priors exist but where strong specifications are not possible. The techniques to be presented have been developed to deal with problems (such as the standing of European public opinion within a larger system of East-West relations) which appear to fall within this intermediate range. Considerations of space prevent a more detailed presentation of this approach to regression.

*A simple thought experiment can bring out the distinction involved here. Assume that the regression weights in an equation were to be artificially changed so that the signs and relative magnitudes of weights varied but the net results, in terms of R^2 and the fit between actual and estimated values, did not change to any great degree. For present purposes, these alterations in the equation would not have any analytical consequences, since the fit between one pattern and some set of other patterns (considered as a set) is the only point emphasized. Obviously, this would not be the case in a path-analytical approach to regression.

THE CONTOURS OF WESTERN EUROPEAN PUBLIC OPINION

Introduction

This section outlines the views of Western European publics which bear directly or indirectly on East-West security relations. It blends a presentation of recent poll results with an analysis of trends. Greater emphasis is placed on the latter element which tends to be neglected and which is the critical aspect for gaining a better understanding of the longer-term dimensions of East-West competition. The section deals with a number of topics: a summary of recent European views on defense subjects; perceptions of East-West competition; preferences regarding superpower parity and how these preferences have changed over time; and an assessment of trends in public perceptions of the military balance and opinions of the superpowers.

The last subject will provide the basis for an examination of the standing of Western European public opinion in the broader context of postwar East-West relations. To the extent possible, the analysis in this section will identify the views of the most highly educated component of the publics, as well as those of the public at large, since the former group is likely to contain many of the opinion leaders whose views are likely to have greater policy import. For convenience (and to provide synonyms) the terms "views," "opinions," "attitudes," and "perceptions" will be used interchangeably.

Recent Survey Results

The most recent (March 1977) views of European publics regarding Soviet and American military strength are presented in Table 6.1. Perceived trends in Soviet and American military strength are presented in Table 6.2.

On the face of things, these are not ideal results from an American perspective. Neither the current standings nor the perceived trends favor the U.S. At the same time, however, attaching strategic import to these results is not an unambiguous matter. Consider, for example, the case of two American analysts, one an adherent of the Assured-Destruction school of strategic thinking and the other a believer in counterforce (and/or damage limitation). To the former, these would be reasonably acceptable standings, since the only point of crucial import would be the percentages who perceived a substantial Soviet lead. To someone in the opposite camp, the results would be much more negative, since more importance would be attached to the large percentages in the "USSR somewhat ahead" category in

TABLE 6.1

U.S.-USSR Military Strength: 1977 Polling Data

"How do you think the U.S. and the USSR compare at the present time
in total military strength—U.S. considerably ahead, U.S. somewhat
ahead, U.S. and USSR about equal, USSR somewhat ahead, USSR
considerably ahead?"

March 1977	Great Britain	France	West Germany
No. of cases	1903	993	1008
U.S. considerably ahead (%)	3 ⎤	6 ⎤	3 ⎤
U.S. somewhat ahead (%)	7 ⎦ 10	10 ⎦ 16	12 ⎦ 15
U.S. and USSR about equal (%)	19	27	35
USSR somewhat ahead (%)	34 ⎤	27 ⎤	25 ⎤
USSR considerably ahead (%)	16 ⎦ 50	7 ⎦ 34	9 ⎦ 34
No opinion (%)	22	23	17
Totals	101%	100%	101%
Net U.S. ahead	-40%	-18%	-19%

Note: Here and in subsequent tables, totals range between 99%
and 101% due to rounding approximation.
Source: United States Advisory Commission on Information
(USACI), The 28th Report (Washington, D.C.: USACI, 1977), p. 183.

Table 6.1. Here, as elsewhere, the meaning of the poll results
depends, to a large extent, on the other factors and considerations.

Perceptions of East-West Competition

There is considerable evidence that European publics (and
leaders as well) do not view East-West competition solely (or perhaps
even primarily) in military terms. In 1972, general and university-
educated publics were asked the question presented in Table 6.3.
Since more than two alternatives were presented, the item is not
strictly comparable to the more recent military-strength question

TABLE 6.2

Shifts in U. S. -USSR Military Strength:
1977 Polling Data

"Regardless of how you believe the U. S. and the USSR compare in
military strength at the present time, do you see military strength
currently shifting more toward the U. S. , more toward the USSR,
or in neither direction?"

March 1977	Great Britain	France	West Germany
No. of cases	1903	993	1008
Toward U. S. (%)	9	11	9
Toward USSR (%)	38	26	32
Neither (%)	28	24	33
No opinion (%)	26	39	27
Totals	101%	100%	101%
Net favorable to U. S.	−29%	−15%	−23%

Source: United States Advisory Commission on Information
(USACI), The 28th Report (Washington, D. C. : USACI, 1977), p. 183.

presented in Table 6.1. Nevertheless, publics can still be compared
by subtracting those who saw the USSR in first place from those who
put the United States in that position.

In the same survey, a more general national power question
was asked which was not restricted to military factors (Table 6.4).

In each country, and for both sets of publics, the U. S. is seen
as being stronger when all of the bases of power are considered than
when the U. S. -USSR comparison is focused—as in Table 6.3—only
on military considerations. When the respondents who put the United
States into first place were asked why they did so, the modal response
attributed the United States' lead to economic rather than military
factors, though the two were quite close in the case of West
Germany. [7]

Another dimension of the perceptions of East-West competition
has to do with expectations of conflict. Some nonsurvey data on this
subject can be taken from the research of Goldmann. [8] Goldmann
uses content analysis to estimate leaders' perceptions of the likelihood

TABLE 6.3

Military Strength: 1972 Polling Data

"Now, which of the countries on this card would you say is the strongest <u>militarily</u> at the present time: U. S. , Soviet Union, Mainland China (PRC), Japan, European Common Market Countries (as a group)?"

(percentages)

	United Kingdom	France	West Germany
General public			
U.S. ahead	29	47	50
USSR ahead	45	28	31
Net favorable to U.S.	−16	+19	+19
University educated			
U.S. ahead	38	59	55
USSR ahead	39	27	34
Net favorable to U.S.	−1	+32	+21

Source: United States Information Agency, <u>U.S. Standing in Foreign Public Opinion Following the President's Visit to China</u> (Washington, D.C.: USIA, 1972), pp. 16, 30.

of interbloc conflict in Europe. Since the early to mid-1960s, leaders' perceptions (as measured by Goldmann) have been favorable, indicating that interbloc conflict is perceived as being less likely. Goldmann's conclusions are consistent with the findings of Lerner and Gordon that only a small fraction of the Western European elites in their surveys anticipated major interbloc war and that the primary Soviet challenge perceived by these leaders was political. [9]

These findings concerning Europeans' expectations of conflict between the blocs and their evaluation of the competition as a predominantly political context bear on the earlier survey results having to do with U.S. and Soviet national power. Clearly, there is an irreducible military component to the relationship between the blocs. At the same time, however, if one regards East-West competition as a long-haul process in which conflict is not anticipated over the shorter term, then the political-economic and political-military components

TABLE 6.4

Overall Strength: 1972 Polling Data

"Considering all the things that make a country strong, what country would you say is the strongest in the world at the present time?"

(percentages)

	United Kingdom	France	West Germany
General public			
U. S.	46	61	59
USSR	29	16	22
Net favorable to U. S.	+17	+45	+37
University educated			
U. S.	50	73	64
USSR	27	8	23
Net favorable to U. S.	+23	+65	+41

Source: United States Information Agency, U.S. Standing in Foreign Public Opinion Following the President's Visit to China (Washington: USIA, 1972), pp. 16, 30.

of the competition take on greater relative importance, if only because they provide the resources required for future military efforts. Viewed in this light, the finding that American standing vis-à-vis the USSR increases when all of the bases of power are considered and that economic factors figure prominently in this evaluation takes on increased relevance and qualifies, to some extent, more narrow evaluations of the comparative military balance, such as those presented in Tables 6.1 and 6.3.

Views of Superpower Parity

From 1958 through 1971, there was a striking shift in the opinion of Western European publics concerning Soviet-American parity. In 1958, a majority of respondents in the United Kingdom and the Federal Republic of Germany and a plurality in France preferred a U.S. lead in military strength (Table 6.5). By 1971, a majority in

TABLE 6.5

U.S.–USSR Military/Nuclear Strength: Polling Preferences

1971 wording: "What would be best in your opinion—for the U.S. to be ahead in nuclear weapons, the Soviet Union to be ahead, or neither to be ahead?"

1964 wording: "What would be best in your opinion—for the U.S. to be ahead in military strength, the Soviet Union to be ahead, or neither to be ahead?"

1958 wording: "Would you prefer the U.S. to be militarily stronger than the USSR, weaker, or about the same in military strength?"

	Great Britain			France			West Germany		
	Oct. 1958	Feb. 1964	July 1971	Oct. 1958	Feb. 1964	July 1971	Oct. 1958	Feb. 1964	July 1971
No. of cases	611	1178	1240	635	1175	1263	610	1202	1211
Prefer U.S. ahead (%)	69	40	31	43	22	12	73	49	31
Prefer USSR ahead (%)	2	1	3	3	2	3	1	–	1
Prefer neither ahead (%)	21	47	56	36	64	71	15	35	56
No opinion (%)	8	12	11	18	12	15	11	16	13
	100%	100%	101%	100%	100%	101%	100%	100%	101%
Net favorable to U.S. (U.S. ahead less USSR ahead plus neither)	46%	-8%	-28%	4%	-44%	-62%	57%	14%	-26%

Source: United States Advisory Commission on Information (USACI), The 28th Report (Washington, D.C.: USACI, 1977), p. 123.

TABLE 6.6

Removal of Missiles

"Some people say that the U.S. should remove its nuclear missiles from bases near the Soviet Union, just as the Soviet Union removed its nuclear missiles from Cuba, near the U.S. Others say that the two cases are quite different, and the U.S. should not remove its missiles. With which of these views are you more inclined to agree?"

	Britain	France	West Germany
No. of cases	1186	1200	1202
Remove U.S. nuclear missiles from bases near the Soviet Union	49%	45%	29%
Don't remove U.S. nuclear missiles	22	19	34
Qualified answer	—	—	2
Don't know	11	20	24
Total	82%	84%	89%
Not aware of crisis	18%	16%	11%

Source: R. L. Merritt and D. J. Puchala, Western European Perspective on International Affairs (New York: Praeger, 1968), p. 448.

all three nations preferred for neither superpower to be ahead in nuclear weapons. This shift in opinion is even more noteworthy because the questions used to identify it are among the few items in the USIA surveys which index policy preferences ("what would be best in your opinion?") rather than state-of-the-world assessments ("who is ahead?").

The February 1963 preference of publics in France and Great Britain for "parity" of another sort between the superpowers is shown in Table 6.6. It is probably no coincidence that the two nations in which a plurality of the respondents favored a parallel removal of American missiles were also the two states which had pluralities in favor of parity in Soviet and American military strength as early as 1964 (see Table 6.5).

Trends in European Assessments of the Military
Balance and Opinions of the Superpowers

Since the mid-1950s, USIA polls have repeated several items a
sufficient number of times to allow for time-series analysis (though
there are some notable gaps in the time series). The most salient
items for present purposes are three questions having to do with
assessments of the military balance and general opinions of the superpowers: "All things considered, which country do you think is ahead
in total military strength at the present time—the United States or
the USSR"? "Do you have a very good, good, neither good nor bad,
bad, or very bad opinion of the USSR?" "Do you have a very good,
good, neither good nor bad, bad, or very bad opinion of the United
States?" The responses of the European publics are plotted in
Figures 6.1 and 6.2. Following the practice of the USIA report
from which these data were taken, net standing scores are presented
in the figures and employed in subsequent analyses. The net standing
score for the balance item is: U.S. ahead minus USSR ahead. The
net standings for the last two items are computed by subtracting the
bad and very bad responses from the good and very good.

The most significant items for present purposes are the
military-balance questions plotted in Figure 6.1. While there are
significant discontinuities in the time series (for example, the
1966-67 and post-69 values), some trends can be identified. The
profiles of opinion are remarkably similar across the three countries.
Assessments of relative American military strength were lowest in
1960-61, the period of the Berlin crisis. Evaluations of relative
U.S. strength increased in all three countries after 1962, possibly
as a result of the missile crisis.

The Germans were consistently the most optimistic concerning
the United States' standing vis-à-vis the USSR; the British were
consistently the most pessimistic.

Turning to public evaluations of the superpowers (Figure 6.2),
other trends can be identified despite missing data. In all three
nations, opinions of the U.S. were always more favorable than views
of the USSR. The West Germans tended to regard the superpowers
in the most extreme terms; the French were most often in the middle,
with neither extremely favorable nor extremely unfavorable
assessments.

Tables 6.7 and 6.8 present the correlations of the three public
opinion items within and between nations. Opinions tended to be
fairly congruent across nations, particularly for assessments of the
military balance and views of the Soviet Union (Table 6.7). A
striking point in Table 6.8 is that the correlation between opinions
of the Soviet Union and opinions of the United States were positive

FIGURE 6.1

Opinion of U. S. -USSR Military Balance

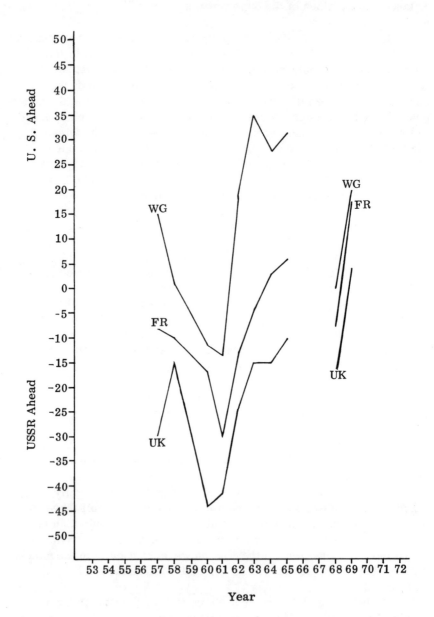

Source: United States Information Agency, <u>Trends in Foreign Attitudes Towards the United States' Role in World Affairs</u> (Washington, D.C.: USIA, 1973), p. A-10.

FIGURE 6. 2

Opinion of Superpowers

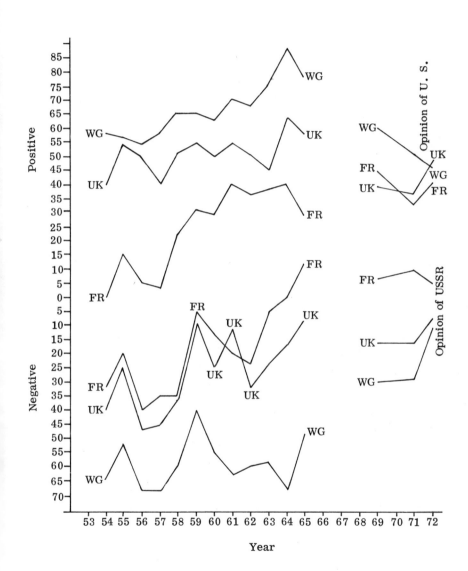

Source: United States Information Agency, Trends in Foreign Attitudes Towards the United States' Role in World Affairs (Washington, D. C. : USIA, 1973), pp. A-1, A-6.

TABLE 6.7

Across-Nation Correlations

	UKoB	FRoB	WGoB
UKoB	1.00	.90	.66
FRoB	—	1.00	.73
WGoB	—	—	1.00
	UKoSU	FRoSU	WGoSU
UKoSU	1.00	.87	.61
FRoSU	—	1.00	.70
WGoSU	—	—	1.00
	UKoUS	FRoUS	WGoUS
UKoUS	1.00	.30	.61
FRoUS	—	1.00	.41
WGoUS	—	—	1.00

Note: The first two letters in each variable code refer to the country (UK = United Kingdom; FR = France; WG = West Germany); the "o" stands for opinion; the last letter or letters refer to the type of opinion (B = of the military balance; SU = of the Soviet Union; US = of the U.S.). Hence, UKoB refers to British public opinion regarding the military balance between the U.S. and USSR. N = 15 observations for oSU and oUS variables; N = 10 for oB variables. All correlations are computed using pair-wise deletion. The use of tests of statistical significance with non sample data is a subject of controversy.

Source: Author's calculations based on data contained in Figures 6.1 and 6.2.

in two of the three nations (with West Germany being the exception). Apparently, the British and French publics did not view the super-powers in simple zero-sum terms, that is, with improving assessments of the one being accompanied by declining assessments of the other. It should be recalled, however, that in all three nations the U.S. was regarded more favorably over the entire period surveyed (see Figure 6.2).

TABLE 6.8

Within-Nation Correlations

	UKoB	UKoSU	UKoUS
UKoB	1.00	.24	-.13
UKoSU	—	1.00	.35
UKoUS	—	—	1.00
	FRoB	FRoSU	FRoUS
FRoB	1.00	.62	.10
FRoSU	—	1.00	.70
FRoUS	—	—	1.00
	WGoB	WGoSU	WGoUS
WGoB	1.00	.19	.38
WGoSU	—	1.00	-.51
WGoUS	—	—	1.00

Note: $N = 15$ for correlations between oSU and oUS; $N = 9$ for correlations involving oB and oSU or oUS (1968 data are available for oB but not for the other two variables).

Source: Author's calculations based on data contained in Figures 6.1 and 6.2.

PUBLIC OPINION IN CONTEXT

This section examines Western European public opinion within the broader context of the system of East-West competition that has existed since World War II. The first portion examines some of the potential influences upon the course taken by public evaluations of the Soviet-American military balance (Figure 6.1). The second part assesses Western European public opinion as one potential influence upon national defense efforts (defense burdens: defense expenditures/ GDP). These national defense efforts, in turn, affect the East-West military balance.

The analyses to be presented in this section are exploratory. Relatively weak theoretical priors and trends are being used. The complexity of the relationships which public opinion has with other factors is undoubtedly being underestimated. As was noted in the first section of this chapter, in these analyses emphasis is placed on

similarities in patterns across variables, using covariation as an
indicator of potential interdependence in a complex system.

Other Elements in the Pattern of
East-West Competition

Previous analyses have identified a number of facets of East-
West relations which might be related to European public opinion. [10]
These factors can be grouped into five sets: (1) the articulated
perceptions of Soviet and U. S. leaders regarding the state of East-
West relations; (2) comparable perceptions for the leaders of the
three Western European nations; (3) the state of the U. S.-USSR
strategic balance; (4) the behaviors directed by the USSR to the three
Western European states; (5) the behaviors exchanged between the
superpowers.

The first two sets of factors will be indexed by using data
collected by Goldmann. [11] Goldmann uses content analysis to assess
the amount of tension in East-West relations in Europe that was
perceived by leaders in NATO and Warsaw Treaty Organization
states.

Based on an interpretation of Goldmann's arguments concerning
the Soviet-American strategic relationship between the superpowers,
the third factor will be identified and distinguished in terms of the
amount of "objective" tension each represented insofar as a stable/
secure nuclear balance was concerned: Phase 1 (1946-47)—3
(Objective Tension Score); Phase 2 (1948-56)—2; Phase 3 (1957-65)—
4; Phase 4 (1966-75)—1.

In this scheme, a low number indexes a low level of objective
tension in the strategic balance. In this sense the most balanced
period was the phase of mutual second-strike capabilities (parity),
1966-75. The next most stable phase was 1948-56, when only the
United States possessed the capability to attack the other superpower's
homeland with a major strategic strike. This was followed by the
period in which neither superpower possessed significant nuclear
forces. Finally, the period which had the most objectively "tense"
or "unstable" relationship was 1957-65, when both superpowers had
counter-homeland nuclear-strike capabilities, but where the U. S.
had a significant lead. Parity, achieved sometime during the mid-
1960s, ended this imbalance. This aspect of the relationship between
the superpowers will be indexed by the four values which follow each
of the phases.

The final two sets of factors will be indexed by using event
data taken from Azar and Sloan. [12] Two types of behaviors

will be considered: conflictual events and "cooperative"
events. *

Potential Influences Upon Public Views
of the Soviet-American Balance

The first analytical question has to do with the potential
influences upon the course of public views of the balance in the three
Western European nations. Table 6.9 shows the correlations between
public views and the potential causal factors identified above.

The results presented in Table 6.9 show that the opinions of
Western European publics regarding the U.S.-USSR military balance
varied over time in ways that were congruent with changes in other
facets of the hypothesized network of East-West competition.
Articulated U.S. perceptions are salient in all three nations. †
Soviet perceptions of tensions are salient in France and West Germany.
National leaders' perceptions are significant in Great Britain and
France. The signs of all of these relationships are positive, with
"better" public views of the balance (better U.S. standings) being
associated with periods in which leaders perceived less tension in
East-West relations in Europe.

The "objective" status of the strategic balance is correlated
with "subjective" impressions of the overall military balance in two
of the three nations (Great Britain and France). The sign of this
correlation reflects the scoring of the strategic balance variable in
which "unstable" periods have higher values.

U.S. conflictual behavior towards the USSR (primarily verbal)
was salient in France and Great Britain. The negative sign of the

---

*It is generally easier to identify conflict rather than coopera-
tion. Some of the events included on the Azar-Sloan cooperation
scale (and other scales of cooperative behaviors) could be interpreted
as indexes of interaction or participation rather than cooperation
per se. In this paper, the Azar-Sloan "cooperation" scale will be
employed as a measure of nonconflictual "activity" (hence the sub-
script "a") since it includes cooperative as well as more neutral interactive behaviors. The yearly mean levels presented in Azar and
Sloan will be employed in the analyses. Where no value is presented
for a given nation and a year, a score of "8" (neutral or indifferent
behaviors) will be assigned on both scales.

†In this study, correlations greater than or equal to .30 in
magnitude will be considered to have substantive significance or
salience.

TABLE 6.9

Correlations of Opinions Concerning
Military Balance and Predictors

	UKoB	FRoB	WGoB
USp	.60	.72	.83
SUp	.27	.46	.48
UKp	.69	—	—
FRp	—	.60	—
WGp	—	—	.20
BLNCE	-.52	-.46	.04
US-SUc	-.71	-.72	-.21
US-SUa	.21	.11	-.18
SU-USc	.02	.00	.34
SU-USa	-.40	-.27	-.15
SU-UKc	-.15	—	—
SU-UKa	.07	—	—
SU-FRc	—	-.52	—
SU-FRa	—	-.53	—
SU-WGc	—	—	.40
SU-WGa	—	—	.72

Key: p = Elite Perception Data; BLNCE = US–USSR Balance
Variable; Behavior Variables = Actor, Target, Type (for example,
US–SUc = U.S. conflictual behaviors toward the USSR, US–SUa
= U.S. cooperative behaviors toward the USSR).

Source: Author's calculations based on data contained in
Figure 6.1, in E. Azar and T. J. Sloan, Dimensions of Interaction:
A Sourcebook for the Study of the Behavior of 31 Nations from
1948 through 1973 (Pittsburgh: International Studies Association,
1975); and in Kjell Goldmann, Tension and Détente in Bipolar
Europe (Stockholm: Esselte Studium/Scandinavian University
Books, 1974).

TABLE 6.10

Multiple Regression Results:
UKoB, FRoB, WGoB

	R	R^2	SEE	F	DW
UKoB	.78	.61	11.0	3.1	2.45
FRoB	.85	.73	8.2	5.6	1.56
WGoB	.90	.82	8.6	9.1	1.19

All equations estimated for the range of the dependent
variable

Source: Author's calculations based on data contained in
Figure 6.1, in E. Azar and T. J. Sloan, Dimensions of Interaction:
A Sourcebook for the Study of the Behavior of 31 Nations From 1948
through 1973 (Pittsburgh: International Studies Association, 1975);
and in Kjell Goldmann, Tension and Détente in Bipolar Europe (Stockholm: Esselte Studium/Scandinavian University Books, 1974).

relationship associates periods of greater U.S. conflict with periods
of greater relative Soviet leads in the perceived balance. The views
of West German publics were positively associated with Soviet
conflict towards the United States. With only three nations involved
in the comparisons, it is difficult to account for national differences
in the salience and signs of individual predictor factors.

Soviet behaviors towards Western European nations were significantly associated with public views of the balance in France and
West Germany. Once again, with only three nations in the comparisons, it is difficult to account for the anomalous signs of the German
correlations.

In terms of the methodological strategy that has been adopted
for this study, the most interesting way in which to examine the standing of Western European public opinion within the larger structure of
East-West competition is to use multiple-regression analysis to
determine if the course of public opinion concerning the balance can
be accurately reproduced on the basis of some set of other factors.
Because of the limited number of degrees of freedom available,
small sets of predictors will be employed. USp was salient in all

FIGURE 6.3

UKoB Results

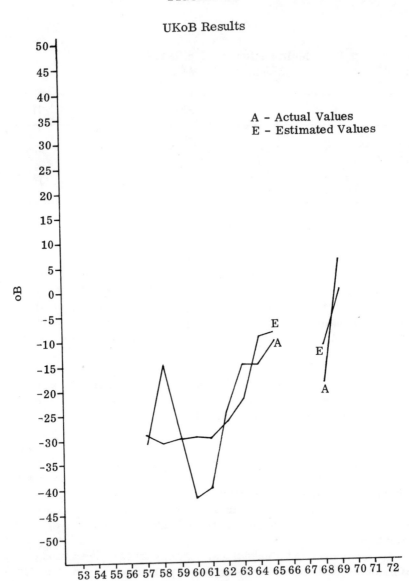

Source: Author's calculations based on data contained in Figure 6.1, in E. Azar and T. J. Sloan, <u>Dimensions of Interaction: A Sourcebook for the Study of the Behavior of 31 Nations From 1948 through 1973</u> (Pittsburgh: International Studies Association, 1975); and in Kjell Goldmann, <u>Tension and Détente in Bipolar Europe</u> (Stockholm: Esselte Studium/Scandinavian University Books, 1974).

FIGURE 6.4

FRoB Results

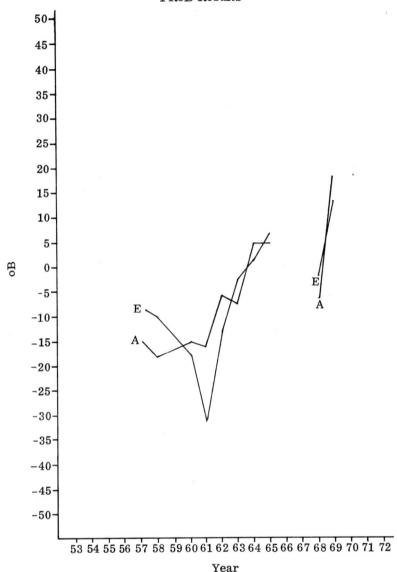

Source: Author's calculations based on data contained in
Figure 6.1, in E. Azar and T. J. Sloan, Dimensions of Interaction:
A Sourcebook for the Study of the Behavior of 31 Nations From 1948
through 1973 (Pittsburgh: International Studies Association, 1975);
and in Kjell Goldmann, Tension and Détente in Bipolar Europe (Stockholm: Esselte Studium/Scandinavian University Books, 1974).

FIGURE 6.5

WGoB Results

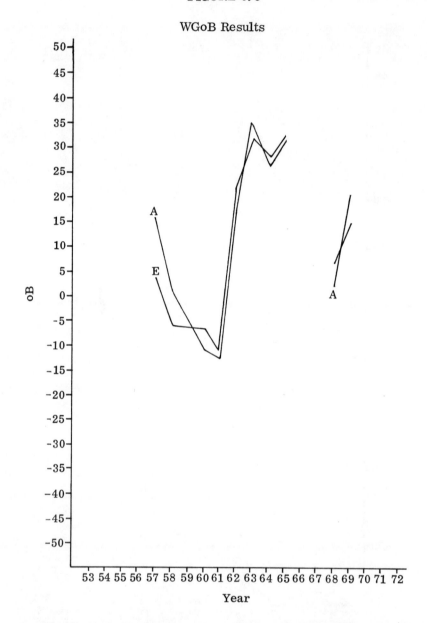

Year

Source: Author's calculations based on data contained in
Figure 6.1, in E. Azar and T. J. Sloan, Dimensions of Interaction:
A Sourcebook for the Study of the Behavior of 31 Nations From 1948
through 1973 (Pittsburgh: International Studies Association, 1975);
and in Kjell Goldmann, Tension and Détente in Bipolar Europe (Stockholm: Esselte Studium/Scandinavian University Books, 1974).

three nations and will be used in all equations. The British and
French equations will also include BLNCE and US–SUc. These
predictors were salient in both nations. Their inclusion provides
a balanced set of predictors reflecting psychological, relational,
and behavioral factors. The West German equation will consist of
USp, and SU–WGa and SU–USc. This provides a mix of one psychological factor plus two types of behavior. The results of the multiple-
regression analyses are provided in Table 6.10 and Figures 6.3,
6.4, and 6.5.

Given the constraints under which the analysis operates, the
results are quite favorable. The course of public views concerning
the balance appears to be reasonably well connected with other facets
of the hypothesized system of East–West competition; the pattern of
public opinion can be reproduced on the basis of the other factors.
The British equation is the weakest. The oscillations in the 1958–
61 period of the Berlin Crisis are underestimated (1961 is a bad
year for the French equation as well). Otherwise the fit between
estimated and actual patterns is respectable. The F levels for the
equations are also respectable.

Public Opinion and the Military Balance

The first half of the section singled out public opinion as a
dependent variable, potentially influenced by a variety of other
factors. The remaining portion of the section will deal with
European public opinion as a potential causative factor, as one of
many possible influences upon the military balance. The postulated
relationship is one in which opinions of the Soviet Union and of the
military balance influence publics' willingness to support national
defense efforts. Changes in public support for defense efforts, in
turn, can influence the balance by affecting resource–allocation
decisions. Opinions of the Soviet Union and views of the balance have
been selected because of their apparent face–validity as potential
influences on support for defense spending. National defense efforts
will be assessed as defense burdens (defense expenditures/gross
domestic product). The course of national defense burdens since the
early 1950s is given in Figure 6.6 and Table 6.11.

German defense expenditures differ markedly from those of
France and Great Britain. The German curve is significantly lower
and flatter. This difference is probably due to a number of factors:
Germany's disarmed status in the early 1950s, the relative size of
the German GDP, and the lack of strategic weapons and forces.
Whatever the precise causes, this German difference appears to
have consequences for later analyses of the influences that might act

FIGURE 6.6

Defense Burdens

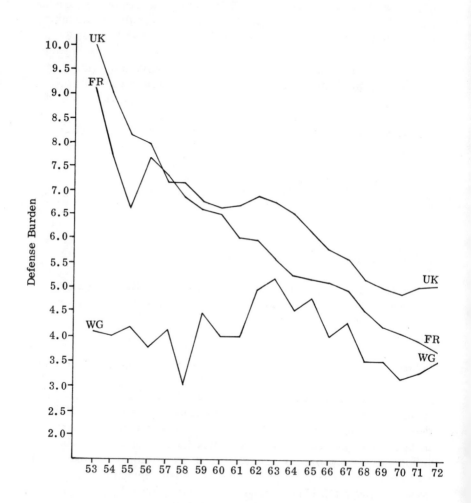

Source: Stockholm International Peace Research Institute, World Armaments and Disarmament (Cambridge: MIT Press, 1975).

122

TABLE 6.11

Correlations of European Defense Burdens

	UKdb	FRdb	WGdb
UKdb	1.00	.92	.18
FRdb	—	1.00	.22
WGdb	—	—	1.00

Source: Author's calculations based on data contained in Figure 6.6.

upon national defense burdens (see below). Reproducing the pattern of earlier analyses, Table 6.12 presents the correlations of oSU and oB with defense burdens.

The similarities in pattern are striking; all of the correlations are above the .30-threshold being employed in the analysis. The negative signs on the correlations mean that national defense burdens decreased as opinions of the USSR became relatively more favorable, and/or as the United States' perceived relative standing in the military balance improved. As before, the Germans present the only anomalous case: the positive correlation between WGoB and WGdb. This may be due to the different form taken by Germany's defense burden since the early 1950s. Multiple-regression results for these variables are presented in Table 6.13 and Figures 6.7, 6.8, and 6.9.

National defense efforts are undoubtedly influenced by many factors in addition to public opinion (for example, the effects of bureaucratic inertia and incremental decision making and the actions of the superpowers). Even so, the patterns of national defense burdens can be accurately reproduced from knowledge of public views concerning the Soviet Union and the U.S.-USSR military balance. All three equations perform well. Interestingly, in light of differences highlighted previously, the fit is weakest for the West German equation.

CONCLUSION: PUBLIC OPINION AND MILITARY POLICY

For the reasons outlined in the first section, the analyses presented in this paper have been exploratory. They have been based upon a relatively weak base of theory and previous research. Even so, on the basis of the results presented, we can come to some

TABLE 6.12

Correlations of European Opinion
and Defense Burdens

	UKob	FRoB	WGoB	UKoSU	FRoSU	WGoSU
UKdb	-.59	—	—	-.68	—	—
FRdb	—	-.64	—	—	-.88	—
WGdb	—	—	+.59	—	—	-.37

Source: Author's calculations based on data contained in
Figures 6.1, 6.2, and 6.6.

TABLE 6.13

Multiple Regression Results:
UKdb, FRdb, WGdb

	R	R^2	F	SEE	D-W
UKdb	.84	.72	7.7	.40	2.00
FRdb	.90	.81	13.4	.45	2.15
WGdb	.71	.51	3.1	.51	1.54

Source: Author's calculations based on data contained in
Figures 6.1, 6.2, and 6.6.

tentative conclusions regarding the bearing which Western European
public opinion has for military policy.

The second section presented a number of significant trends
and changes in the views of Western European publics regarding
such factors as the desirability of U.S.-USSR parity, assessments
of the two superpowers, and views of the military balance. Some of
the more significant findings were that:

● In recent polls, substantial percentages of Western European
publics perceive the Soviets as having an edge in the military
balance, with the significance of this perceived lead being

FIGURE 6.7

UKdb Results

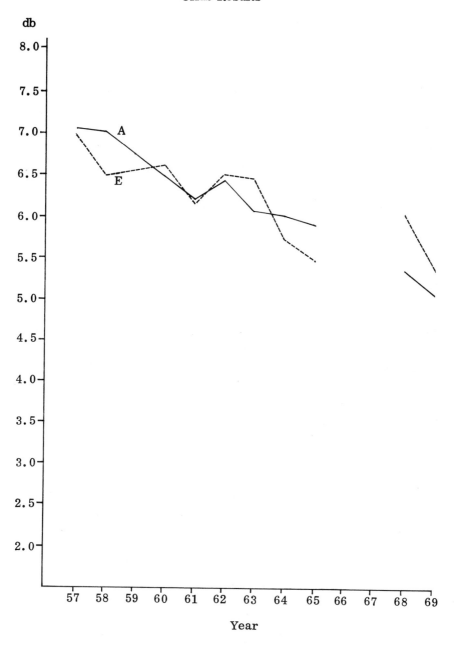

Source: Author's calculations based on data contained in Figures
6.1, 6.2, and 6.6.

FIGURE 6.8

FRdb Results

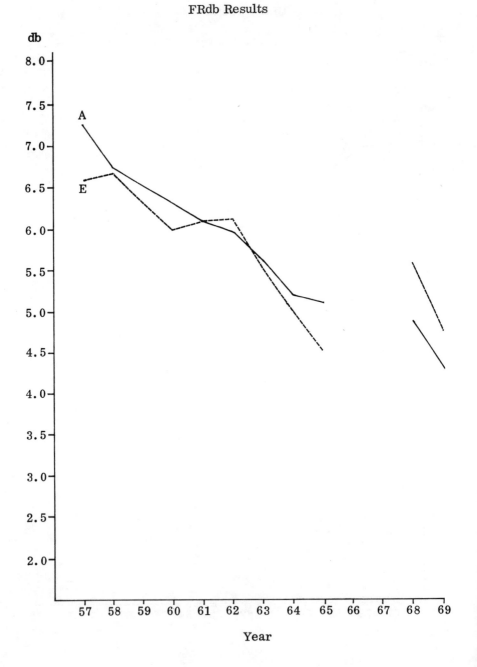

Source: Author's calculations based on data contained in
Figures 6.1, 6.2, and 6.6.

126

FIGURE 6.9

WGdb Results

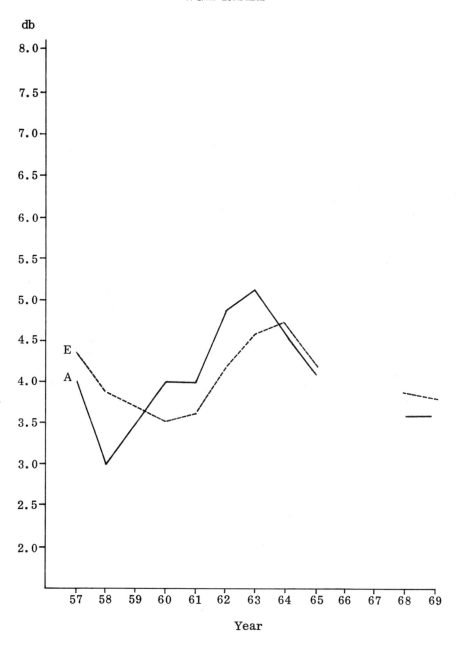

Source: Author's calculations based on data contained in
Figures 6.1, 6.2, and 6.6.

127

highly conditioned by the strategic theory within which it is viewed.

- The United States fares much better in comparisons in which all bases of national power (rather than simply military factors) are considered; it was further argued that this was a reasonable perception if East-West competition is considered as a long-haul process in which conflict is not anticipated over the shorter term.

- There have been striking shifts in the views of Western European publics regarding the desirability of parity; recent survey results show a strong stand in favor of U. S. -USSR parity instead of a U. S. lead; these findings are even more significant because the items which index them are among the few poll questions which focus on policy preferences.

The study's most significant finding is that trends in public assessments of the superpower balance and views of the USSR covary to a substantial extent with other facets of East-West relations. This was true both when public views were considered as a dependent variable—potentially influenced by a variety of other factors—and when the potential influence of public opinion upon national defense burdens was examined. This pattern of moderate to strong covariation supports the earlier assumptions and arguments that public opinion within Western European nations plays a role in the larger system of East-West competition, both as an influence and as a subject of influence. In turn, this lends support to recent tendencies within the U. S. analytical communities to take a broader view of American political-military affairs (as opposed to a focus confined strictly to military factors) and to direct more analytical attention to the broader policy context of factors such as public opinion within which U. S. defense policy is formulated and implemented.

NOTES

1. G. Arbatov, The War of Ideas in Contemporary International Relations (Moscow: Progress Publishers, 1973), pp. 7-16, 38.

2. D. Tomashevsky, Lenin's Ideas and Modern International Relations (Moscow: Progress Publishers, 1974), pp. 82-83.

3. See, for example, M. Baskakov and Y. Kornilov, Soviet-American Relations: New Prospects (Moscow: Progress Publishers, 1975), p. 64.

4. C. D. Jones, "Just Wars and Limited Wars: Restraints on the Use of the Soviet Armed Forces," World Politics 28 (October 1975), pp. 44-68.

5. Central Intelligence Agency, Biographic Report: USSR Institute of the United States of America and Canada (CR 76-10864, April 1976), p. v.

6. M. Fishbein and I. Ajzen, Belief, Attitude, Intention and Behavior: An Introduction to Theory and Research (Reading, Mass: Addison-Wesley, 1975), passim.

7. R. B. Mahoney Jr. , "An Assessment of Public and Elite Perceptions in France, the United Kingdom, and the Federal Republic of Germany," Professional Paper No. 164 (Arlington, Va: Center for Naval Analyses, 1976), pp. 5, 9.

8. Kjell Goldmann, Tension and Détente in Bipolar Europe (Stockholm: Esselte Studium/Scandinavian University Books, 1974) and Kjell Goldmann and J. Lagerkranz, East-West Tension in Europe, 1971-1975, Updating of a Model (Stockholm: The Swedish Institute of International Affairs, 1977).

9. D. Lerner and M. Gordon, Euratlantica (Cambridge: MIT Press, 1969), p. 1054.

10. R. B. Mahoney, Jr. , "American Political-Military Operations and the Structure of the International System, 1946-1975" (Paper presented at the Meeting of the Section on Military Studies, International Studies Association, Ohio State University, Columbus, October 1976) and R. B. Mahoney, Jr. , "European Perceptions and East-West Competition" (Paper presented at the Annual Meeting of the International Studies Association, St. Louis, Mo. , March 1977).

11. Goldmann, op. cit.

12. E. Azar and T. J. Sloan, Dimensions of Interaction: A Source Book for the Study of the Behavior of 31 Nations From 1948 Through 1973 (Pittsburgh: International Studies Association, 1975).

7

FRENCH PERCEPTIONS OF THE U.S.-SOVIET MILITARY BALANCES: ANALYSIS OF *DEFENSE NATIONALE*

Donald C. Daniel

INTRODUCTION

This chapter complements the earlier inquiry into public opinion with an analysis of twenty years (1955-74) of Defense Nationale, a journal accepted as representing particularly well the views of French governmental officials and defense-oriented intellectuals. [1]

France is singled out for attention since she is a particularly interesting state to key on regarding third-country perceptions of the U. S. -USSR balances. Historically the most independent of the NATO states in her foreign and military policy, she has probably gone the farthest in generating uncertainties as to her intentions in the event of a major U. S. -USSR or East-West conflict. Her overtures to the Soviet Union (especially during the de Gaulle years), her development of the force de frappe, and her withdrawal from the military structure of the alliance all provide the basis for hypothesizing that, if French observers viewed the military balances as shifting away from the United States, they might in general be more apt than their NATO colleagues to recommend policies calling for greater aloofness from the Americans or closer accommodation with the Soviet Union.

This research was supported by the Advanced Research Projects Agency of the Department of Defense and was monitored by Gerald Sullivan and Robert Young under Contract No. 3117. The conclusions contained in this study are those of the author and should not be interpreted as necessarily representing the official policies, either expressed or implied, of the Naval Postgraduate School, ARPA, or any other agency of the U. S. Government.

DÉFENSE NATIONALE

According to its masthead, Défense Nationale (referred to
hereafter as DN) inquires into the "great national and international
questions," be they "military, economic, political, scientific." It is
a highly respected journal published by the Comité d'études de défense
nationale, an organization somewhat akin to the Council on Foreign
Relations of the United States. Its authors often consist of French
government and military officials, including ministers and military
chiefs-of-staff.

The journal appeared 11 times a year, and a total of 219 were
published from 1955 through 1974. In 1968 one normally expected
issue failed publication, but the editors made up for it by increasing
the content of several succeeding issues. The only year for which
statistical totals are not fully comparable with those of others is
1964 since the July number was missing from the serial collection
to which the writer had access.

Each journal contained approximately 175 pages and contained
about 10 articles and 25 to 30 "Chronicle" items ("c.i.'s"). Articles
accounted for approximately two-thirds of any one journal. As
suggested by the masthead, they did not exclusively deal with
military or defense questions but also with a wide variety of other
topics such as syndicalism, the United Arab Republic after Nasser,
meteorological satellites, or the relation between salaries, prices,
and unemployment. Items found in the "Chronicle" section took up
about one-fourth of each journal. Their purpose was to keep readers
informed of current developments in national and international
military, naval, maritime, and aeronautical affairs as well as NATO,
international organization, and French overseas matters. Most were
moderate in length while some were no longer than one paragraph
and others were equivalent to or approached full-length articles.
The remainder of each DN issue was devoted to advertisements and
a "Bibliography" section which briefly described recent books of
interest.

STUDY PROCEDURES

Reading Défense Nationale

The writer read DN selectively and scrutinized an article or
c.i. only if it concerned itself with one or more of the following
topics: (1) French policy toward the United States, the Soviet Union,
NATO, or the Soviet Bloc; (2) U.S., Soviet, NATO, or Soviet bloc
policy vis-à-vis one another or France; (3) French weapons

developments, defense policy, military capabilities, or military activities but not as these related to French colonies or Third World nations; (4) U. S. and/or Soviet weapons developments, defense policies, military capabilities, or military activities but not when these were inspired by purposes other than keeping the other superpower's military in check;* (5) the defense of Western Europe as a whole, or Central Europe-West Germany, or of France; (6) control of or hegemony in the various seas or oceans of the world; (7) deterrence, war, military strategy or tactics (as, for example, articles dealing with strategy in the nuclear age) but excluding articles dealing with guerrilla war.

The above criteria were intended to guide the selection process so that only relevant articles or c. i.'s—relevant in the sense of containing military comparisons—would "surface" for investigation. I started with criteria which were vague and refined them in the process of almost cover-to-cover reading of the journals for 1955–56 and 1965–66. That reading, plus further sampling, made it clear that because of consistently low utility one could eliminate from further consideration the "Bibliography" section, the "Overseas" section of the Chronicle, and articles published under the recurring rubrics: "Science and Technology" and "Economic Facts."

The process of selecting articles or c. i.'s for scrutiny began with a review of titles. On that basis alone, some seemed obviously worthy of investigation while others seemed just as obviously irrelevant—the latter being immediately dropped from consideration. Titles on a third group were sufficiently tantalizing or ambiguous to rate reading the introductory and closing paragraphs as well as scanning the material in between. All articles or c. i.'s deemed worthy of investigation were then read to see if they actually did contain balance comparisons. In all, 258 articles and 77 c. i.'s were coded. †

---

*In contrast, excluded from consideration were articles that, for example, dealt with U. S. activities aimed at checking rebel, guerrilla, or insurgent activities in Third World countries or with U. S. aid intended to help Israel check or balance the Arabs.

†Admittedly, both the criteria for selection and the method described above were by no means foolproof. It might have been possible to make the selection process both speedier and less subjective by deciding ahead of time, for example, to read thoroughly every third article or c. i. and code only those balance comparisons which by chance were contained therein. The writer chose not to do that on the conviction that too much relevant data would be lost and that time would be wasted in reading articles, for instance, whose

Coding Défense Nationale

   For the purposes of this chapter, coding Défense Nationale
meant answering six questions. The first was, What military
capabilities are being compared? The categories of concern are
comparisons of:

- overall strategic nuclear capabilities[2]
- strategic bombs and warheads[3]
- strategic missiles (aggregate)[4]
- ballistic-missile submarines[5]
- strategic aviation/strategic bombers[6]
- overall conventional or ground-forces capabilities[7]
- overall naval capabilities[8]
- overall air capabilities[9]

   In the overwhelming majority of cases, there was little
difficulty in deciding under which category a comparison belonged.
For example, authors would simply come out and say something to
the effect that one side had nuclear, conventional, or naval superiority or more and/or better missiles, bombers, ships, and the
like.* Of course, different authors may have had different conceptions as to what they meant by what they said. For example, one
group of authors viewed strategic aviation as entailing only bombers
capable of striking one superpower's homeland by taking off from
the other's, while a second group seemed to consider European-
based U.S. tactical aircraft as strategic bomber assets. In coding,
this writer did not control for such differences since attempting to
do so turned out to be overly complicated and time-consuming.
   Partly for the same reasons, some comparisons of more or less
different capabilities were grouped together in one category. The
"conventional or ground forces" category, for instance, reflected the
oft-recurring situation where DN authors would make general

----

titles or scanning indicated a high probability that they had little or
no value to this study.
   *Because of difficulties in knowing exactly what was being com-
pared, coding for one balance category not mentioned above had to be
discontinued. This category dealt with "general military power/war-
winning capability." There were too many unresolvable, ambiguous
statements in the writings potentially relevant to this category. The
ambiguity arose from constantly recurring references to Soviet or
U.S. power in general which seemed to be military-associated but
were never clear enough to rate coding.

assertions about Soviet conventional superiority but then restrict examples or amplifying data to ground forces only. Because of the difficulty of knowing under what category to code such references (a conventional-forces category or a ground-forces category), and for purposes of simplicity and expediency, this writer chose to form a category uniting both capabilities and coded accordingly.

Sometimes, a more difficult task than categorizing comparisons was deciding if a comparison was intended in the first place. A central concept of this study, the word "balance" ("equilibre" in the French), was itself a source of uncertainty in this regard. At times, the term was used such that it was not clear if the DN author meant that the superpowers were in balance, meaning equal, or whether they were actors in a balance, whatever its actual state might be. For instance, it is not entirely clear how an author views the balance when he writes: "French policy cannot ignore the nuclear balance existing between the superpowers." This writer had to make a careful study of the context in order to decide whether to code such a reference. If nothing in the context suggested that the DN author viewed both sides as equal, then the reference was not coded.

On occasion reference was made to both superpowers in such a way as to place them in a class by themselves, implying a comparison that had them roughly equal. More than one article, for example, contained the admonition that France must continue her force de frappe and related delivery-system programs even though she had no hope of matching U.S. or Soviet capabilities. This writer accepted that, in comparing France with both superpowers, the DN author in a sense was also implying some measure of rough equality between them since they together (rather than just one) set the norm, the standard, against which the French program was being measured.

Once this writer decided that the DN author was making a comparison, that comparison was coded only one time per article or Chronicle item. This coding rule applied no matter how often an author stated in his piece that one or the other side was ahead or equal.

The second question which guided the coding process was, Whose capabilities are being compared? While the main thrust of this study was to reach conclusions about U.S. and Soviet (US-SU) balances, it was thought useful to code comparisons of NATO/West vs. Soviet Union/Soviet bloc (N/W-S/S) conventional military capabilities. So doing helped put into perspective the context in which the conventional balances were viewed since it allowed one to answer questions such as, Is the naval balance viewed more in US-SU or N/W-S/S terms?

The Soviet Union was singled out as an entity on the S/S side since there were many articles or items which specifically compared

NATO or Western capabilities against those of the Soviet Union alone
rather than the Warsaw Pact or Soviet bloc. In contrast, there were
no comparisons involving the United States alone versus the Soviet
bloc/Warsaw Pact. Less than a handful of Soviet comparisons implied
that China was a member of the bloc.

Because the United States and Soviet Union were viewed as
being the undisputed primary competitors in all aspects of strategic
weapons and delivery systems, all comparisons relative to these
systems were coded as US–SU balances. This coding rule applied
regardless of whether the journal author may have referred to "East
versus West" rather than to the superpowers per se when making
strategic-system comparisons.

The third coding question was, Which side does the DN author
see as superior at the time of writing? In this regard, mention has
already been made of those cases where DN authors talked of the
superpowers being in a class by themselves, implying in this writer's
view a comparison that had both equal. There were also instances—
occurring 15 times—when some comparisons had to be coded as "split
opinions" ("s. o. 's"). These occurred either because the authors
were ambiguous or undecided as to whether one side was ahead or
whether equality existed, or because they had one side ahead in some
circumstances and its adversary ahead in others.

An oft-recurring situation—indeed, one which reflected standard
operating procedure in the Chronicles—was for a DN author to quote
or paraphrase without comment someone else's views on a balance.
Since the purpose of this study is to present DN perceptions of the
balances, it did not make sense for this writer to code, for example,
Chairman Khrushchev's or Secretary MacNamara's views if these
were presented in strictly reportorial fashion. Hence, comparisons
were coded only if the DN authors seemed to subscribe or accept
the views in question. Contextual analysis was the method utilized
to resolve ambiguous cases.

Contextual analysis was also utilized to deal with a similar but
relatively infrequent problem—i. e. , resolving ambiguities about
whether an author's statement concerning a balance reflected his
views as to which side was ahead at the time the author was writing.
For example, if an author writing in 1970 stated that the Soviets were
ahead in strategic missiles in 1959 but gave no indication that they
were also superior in 1970, then no comparison was coded.

The fourth and fifth questions in the coding process were simple
to answer. The fourth inquired into whether quantitative factors
played a significant role in perceptions. Coding consisted of noting
those comparisons where numerical measures were explicitly relied
on (either independently or in conjunction with qualitative factors)
in assessments of the balance. Question five entailed noting what

sources were specifically acknowledged by the DN writer as providing him with information about the balance with which he was concerned.

Coding question number six—What recommendations does the DN author make in view of the state of a balance as he perceives it?—required that this writer exercise a fair degree of judgment. The reason is that, while many recommendations were straightforward, causing no coding problems, a large number were not directly linked by the DN author to the comparisons with which they were associated by this writer. It was not at all unusual for a DN author to make comparisons in the course of an argument in which he made a number of other points and assertions. Numerous recommendations might also be made, but none would necessarily be tied in any direct, explicit, "cause-and-effect" manner to any of the points or comparisons made in the argument, yet particular recommendations seemed to this writer to flow logically from the comparisons made and hence were coded. In so doing, care was taken not to make connections which the DN author simply did not intend to have made.

Collating the Data

Collating the data meant ascertaining trends or patterns contained in the coded responses. For the purposes of this chapter, the questions which guided the collating process fall into three groups.

Questions relating to the frequency of comparisons:

● How did the balances rank relative to one another over the 20 years in terms of the frequency in which they appeared?
● If one compares frequency totals for the last two five-year periods, were there any radical shifts in the attention paid each balance where attention is measured by frequency of comparisons?
● Were conventional force comparisons most often made in a US–SU or N/W–S/S context?

Questions relating to DN author perceptions of the balances:

● What were the long-term trends in perceptions? Particularly, which balances over the twenty years trended in favor of perceived U.S. superiority, USSR superiority, or parity?
● What were the more recent trends in perceived superiority or parity if one compares perception totals over the last two five-year periods?

- Were perceptions for the conventional balances in the N/W–
  S/S context similar to those in the U. S. -USSR context?

Questions relating to quantitative indicators:

- How often did quantitative indicators play a role in comparisons?
- Which balance areas most often involved reliance on quantitative
  measures?

Question relating to sources:

- Grouping sources into categories, how did they rank relative
  to one another over the twenty-year period?

Questions relating to DN author policy recommendations:

- If one focuses on policy recommendations having applicability to
  more than one balance area, which recommendations recurred
  most frequently?
- Were these recommendations associated with any recurring or
  predominant views as to which side was ahead in the respective
  balances?
- From this writer's viewpoint, were there any recommendations
  which recurred much less frequently than expected?

STUDY RESULTS

Results Relating to the Frequency of Comparisons

There were 361 comparisons overall, and their distribution in
order of frequency across the balances is contained in Table 7.1.
This table also highlights shifts in attention paid to each balance by
noting the difference in the number of comparisons made in 1965-69
with the number made in 1970-74. As seen therein, the strategic
balances generally received the greatest amount of attention with the
strategic-nuclear balance being by far the subject of the greatest
number of comparisons. Consistent with the frequency of strategic-
nuclear comparisons was the relatively high number of strategic
missile (aggregate) references. Of the conventional balances, the
naval was definitely the most significant while both the air and
conventional-or-ground-forces categories received the smallest
amount of attention of all balance areas.

There were no radical shifts in the attention given to any
balance. The most significant difference in the number of comparisons

TABLE 7.1

Frequency of Comparisons

Balance	Number of Comparisons (1955–74)	Change in Number of Comparisons (1965–69 vs. 1970–74)
(1) Strategic nuclear	201	−2 (From 55 to 57)
(2) Strategic missiles (aggregate)	57	−3 (From 18 to 15)
(3) Naval-in-general	29	+2 (From 4 to 6)
(4) Strategic nuclear bombs and warheads	22	0 (From 7 to 7)
(5) Ballistic-missile submarines	21	−3 (From 8 to 5)
(5) Strategic bombers/ strategic aviation	21	0 (From 7 to 7)
(6) Conventional or ground forces-in-general	6	0 (From 0 to 0)
(7) Air-in-general	4	+1 (From 0 to 1)

Source: Compiled by author.

made in the last two five-year periods was a decrease of three comparisons each associated with both the strategic missile (aggregate) and the ballistic-missile submarine balances.

From the point of view of context (see Table 7.2), the conventional, or ground-forces, balance was most often seen in N/W–S/S terms and the naval in US–SU terms. The air totals were too small for valid conclusions.

Results Relating to DN-Author Perceptions of the Balances

The data summarized in Table 7.3 indicate that over the twenty years of DN publication the United States dominated in comparisons of strategic bombs and warheads, ballistic-missile submarines, strategic aviation, overall naval power, and overall air power—though

TABLE 7. 2

Conventional Balances in
US-SU and N/W-S/S Context

	Number of:	
Balance	US-SU Comparisons	N/W-S/S Comparisons
Conventional or ground forces	6	36
Naval	29	9
Air	4	2

Source: Compiled by author.

the U. S. lead in this last area is questionable due to the small number
of comparisons. The Soviets led in only one category: that of conventional or ground forces, but its lead is also questionable, not only
because of the paucity of comparisons, but also the fact that there
were no comparisons in the period from 1965-74. * Both superpowers
were overwhelmingly perceived as equal in the strategic-nuclear
balance, and both were viewed as superior in a nearly equal number
of times in strategic missiles, this balance being in "stalemate" for
the twenty years as a whole since 86 percent of all comparisons had
one or another side ahead.

Trends of a more recent nature result from comparing perceptions in 1965-69 with those in 1970-74. Table 7. 4 reveals that the
United States in 1970-74 "held its own" in maintaining 1965-69 leads
in strategic bombs and warheads, ballistic missile submarines, and
strategic aviation. In no area, however, did it "experience" a
significant increase in favorable perceptions whether one compares
absolute totals or percentages.

---

*The Soviet lead, however, is not so questionable if one con-
siders that USSR forces make up the vast bulk of Warsaw Pact armies
and that, of 36 N/W-S/S comparisons of conventional or ground
forces, the Soviet group was perceived as superior in every case.
See below, Table 7. 6.

TABLE 7.3

Balance Perceptions, 1955–74

Balance	Favorable to U.S.	Favorable to USSR	Equality	Total
Strategic–nuclear	28 + 2 s.o. (14%)	3 (1%)	168 + 2 s.o. (84%)	120 (99%)
Strategic bombs and warheads	11 + 1 (52%)	3 + 1 (16%)	7 (32%)	22 (100%)
Strategic missile (aggregate)	24 + 4 (46%)	22 + 2 (40%)	7 + 2 (14%)	57 (100%)
Ballistic–missile submarines	14 + 3 (74%)	3 + 3 (21%)	1 (5%)	21 (100%)
Strategic bombers/ strategic aviation	20 (95%)	0 (0%)	1 (5%)	21 (100%)
Conventional or ground forces	0 (0%)	6 (100%)	0 (0%)	6 (100%)
Naval	25 (86%)	0 (0%)	4 (14%)	29 (100%)
Air	3 (75%)	0 (0%)	1 (25%)	4 (100%)

Note: In this and following tables, percentages may not total 100 due to rounding.

Source: Compiled by author.

TABLE 7.4

Balance Perceptions
1965–69 and 1970–74

	1965–69				1970–74			
Balance	Favor-able to U. S.	Favor-able to USSR	Equal-ity	Totals	Favor-able to U. S.	Favor-able to USSR	Equal-ity	Totals
Strategic-nuclear	13 (23%)	0 (0%)	44 (77%)	57 (100%)	5 (9%)	0 (0%)	50 (91%)	55 (100%)
Strategic bombs and warheads	5 (71%)	2 (29%)	0 (0%)	7 (100%)	4 + 1 (64%)	1 + 1 (21%)	1 (14%)	7 (99%)
Strategic missiles (aggregate)	13 + 1 (75%)	1 + 1 (8%)	3 (16%)	18 (99%)	6 + 1 (43%)	6 + 1 (43%)	2 (13%)	15 (99%)
Ballistic-missile submarines	5 + 1 (69%)	1 + 1 (19%)	1 (13%)	8 (101%)	3 + 1 (70%)	1 + 1 (30%)	0 (0%)	5 (100%)
Strategic bombers/ strategic aviation	7 (100%)	0 (0%)	0 (0%)	7 (100%)	7 (100%)	0 (0%)	0 (0%)	7 (100%)
Conven-tional or ground forces	0	0	0	0	0	0	0	0
Naval	4 (100%)	0 (0%)	0 (0%)	4 (100%)	3 (50%)	0 (0%)	3 (50%)	6 (100%)
Air	0	0	0	0	0 (0%)	0 (0%)	1 (100%)	1 (100%)

Source: Compiled by author.

In contrast, the Soviet Union went from being viewed ahead in only 8 percent of 1965-69 strategic missile comparisons to 43 percent in 1970-74—a very sizable gain occurring predominantly at the expense of favorable U.S. perceptions. The end result is that the strategic missile balance shifted from overwhelming U.S. domination in perceptions in the former time period to both superpowers being viewed as ahead an equal number of times in the latter.

An even greater percentage shift took place—again at the expense of perceived US superiority—in the naval balance. There were only four comparisons of overall naval power in 1965-69, but all favored the United States. The number increased to six in the next five years, but only three were "pro-U.S." The remaining three had the balance in parity, causing this balance to trend for the first time in the direction of equality.

The tendency to perceive the strategic nuclear balance as in equality, already well established in 1965-69, was reinforced in 1970-74 as the U.S. lost some ground in this balance also. In the first of these periods, 77 percent of all comparisons had both sides equal and the remaining 23 percent had the U.S. ahead. By the end of the second period, the percentages had changed to 91 and 9 respectively.

As for the air and conventional-or-ground-forces balances, there were too few comparisons to allow for conclusions.

Table 7.5 links together the twenty-year trends with the more recent trends described immediately above. Balances by long-term trend are grouped together in columns while arrows or boxes represent recent trends. An arrow indicates the direction of a significant shift in perceptions while a box signifies that no such shift occurred. A heavy box has been placed around the strategic nuclear balance to highlight the increasing tendency over the last ten years to view it as in equality. Parentheses around the air and conventional-or-ground-forces categories indicate that trends associated with them are of questionable significance due to the small number of comparisons.

In comparing US-SU and N/W-S/S trends, it is best to start with the naval area, where long-term trends for both contexts match because both the US and N/W sides clearly dominated (see Table 7.6). In contrast, the short-term trends are dissimilar since the US-SU context shifted toward equality while the N/W-S/S did not. Lack of adequate data precludes reaching any such conclusions for the other conventional balances. It is worth noting, however, that of the 42 conventional-or-ground-forces comparisons (6 US-SU and 36 N/W-S/S), the Soviet group was perceived as superior in each instance.

TABLE 7.5

Balance Perception Trends

U.S.-Dominated Balances (1955-74)	Equal/Stalemate Balances (1955-74)	USSR-Dominated Balances (1955-74)
Strategic Bombs and Warheads	Strategic Nuclear	(Conventional or Ground Forces*)
Ballistic Missile Submarines		
Strategic Bombers/ Strategic Aviation	Strategic Missiles (Aggregate)	
Overall Naval Power		
(Overall Air Power)(a)		

*Long-term and recent trends are of questionable significance due to insufficient number of comparisons. However, on conventional or ground forces balance, see footnote at bottom of page 130.

Source: Compiled by author.

TABLE 7.6

US–SU Conventional–Balance
Perceptions in N/W–S/S Context

Balance	Favorable to U.S.	Favorable to USSR	Equality	Favorable to N/W	Favorable to S/S	Equality
Conventional or ground forces						
Twenty-year Totals	0	6	0	0	36	0
1965–69 Totals	0	0	0	0	10	0
1970–74 Totals	0	0	0	0	4	0
Naval						
Twenty-year Totals	25	0	4	7 + 1	1	1 + 1
1965–69 Totals	4	0	0	2	0	0
1970–74 Totals	3	0	3	1	0	0
Air						
Twenty-year Totals	3	0	1	0 + 1	1	1 + 1
1965–69 Totals	0	0	0	0	0	0
1970–74 Totals	0	0	1	0	0	0

Source: Compiled by author.

TABLE 7.7

Comparisons Involving Quantitative Measures

Balance	Total of All Comparisons	Number of Comparisons with Quantitative Measures	Percent of Comparisons for Area
Strategic bombs and warheads	22	13	59
Naval-in-general	29	16	55
Strategic aviation	21	10	48
Ballistic-missile submarines	21	8	38
Strategic missiles	57	20	35
Air-in-general	4	1	25
Strategic nuclear	201	16	8
Conventional or ground forces	6	0	0

Source: Compiled by author.

Results Relating to the Use of Quantitative Measures

Quantitative measures entered into 23 percent of all comparisons—that is, in 84 of the 361 assessments. As seen in Table 7.7, DN authors had a very strong tendency to think numerically (whether exclusively or in conjunction with qualitative factors) when contemplating the strategic bombs and warheads, naval, and strategic-aviation balances. For each area 59, 55, and 48 percent respectively of the comparisons were quantitatively oriented either in whole or in part. The strategic-nuclear and conventional-or-ground-forces areas differed sharply since only 8 percent of the former and none of the latter (which had only six comparisons) involved numerical indicators. If one eliminates these last two from consideration, then quantitative factors entered into 44 percent of the remaining assessments.

Results Relating to Sources of Information

DN authors acknowledged the sources they relied on for information about the balances on 82 occasions, and these are grouped

TABLE 7.8

Acknowledged Sources by Group

Source	Number of Acknowledgments	Percent of Acknowledgments
U.S. Government	37	45
(Defense Department)	(35)	(43)
Military force annuals	27	33
(Military Balance)	(15)	(18)
Journals specialized to defense/military matters	8	10
Nonspecialized journals/ newspapers	3	4
Other sources	7	9

Source: Compiled by author.

together in Table 7.8. Contrasting sharply with the fact that no Soviet source was ever mentioned, the United States government (especially the Defense Department) accounted for 46 percent of the acknowledgments—well ahead of any other source. Annual publications specializing in military force levels made up 34 percent with The Military Balance, published by the International Institute for Strategic Studies, alone constituting 19 percent. With the category labeled "other," including two additional references to the IISS as an organization, the result is that the Institute was, after the U.S. government, the second most acknowledged organizational source.

Results Relating to DN Author Recommendations

Three recommendations recurred most frequently. The first was that France or Western Europe should develop a force de frappe and/or related delivery systems. This recommendation appeared 51 times and with increasing frequency in successive five-year periods (that is, 10, 11, 13, and 17 times). It was usually made in

connection with comparisons of the strategic balances in which both
sides were viewed as equal, and it was not at all unusual for it to be
associated with the thought that, due to increases in Soviet strategic
power, the United States could no longer be counted on to go to
nuclear war in response to Soviet aggression in Europe. It was also
not unusual, regardless of the perceived state of a balance, to have
this suggestion justified by claims that France must develop her
deterrent either to avoid a superpower condominium or to assure
herself a strong voice in NATO circles.

Recurring somewhat less frequently (42 times) were admonitions
that the United States and/or the West should increase their flexible-
response capabilities. These recommendations occurred especially
with strategic comparisons that had both sides equal. They also
arose with "pro-SU" conventional-or-ground-forces comparisons
(3) and "pro-US" naval comparisons (2). Unlike the force de frappe
recommendation, this one generally appeared with decreasing
frequency per five-year period (14, 14, 9, and 5 respectively).

Occurring 23 times, and almost always in connection with
strategic balances, were suggestions to the effect that the West
must act to counter Soviet politicopsychological advances in the Third
World. All except one of these recommendations were made in the
late 1950s and early 1960s when Khrushchev was strongly wooing
the underdeveloped and verbally supporting "wars of national
liberation." They were particularly associated with the Soviets'
reaching equality in the strategic areas (hence assuring themselves
a modicum of security vis-à-vis the United States) or with Soviet
space activities viewed as particularly impressive to Third World
states.

Some recommendations were conspicuous by their absence or
by the small number of times they appeared. As perceptions of the
strategic-missile balance shifted strongly away from U. S. domination
to equality in the last five years of the study, one might have expected
that at least some DN writers would have called on the United States
to build up its missile arsenal. Such was not the case. However,
this was not inconsistent with the increased trend of perceiving the
strategic-nuclear balance as equal and the continued tendency to
accept U. S. superiority in strategic bombs and warheads, ballistic-
missile submarines, and strategic aviation. It was also not inconsistent with the belief of many DN authors that both superpowers had
an excess of sufficiency in the strategic nuclear area so that an
increase in such missile numbers would make little difference.
There were merely five recommendations (all reflecting perceived
equality in the strategic-nuclear balance) supporting the SAL
negotiations or agreements and no recommendations, even with the
mutual balanced-force-reduction talks, supporting conventional-

arms-control measures. In contrast to the encouragement given the force de frappe, there was only one occasion (in 1971) when an author called upon France, exclusive of the West or the United States, to build up her conventional force capabilities—in this case, naval (reflecting perceived equality in the naval balance). Finally, while many DN authors desired that France/Western Europe build a nuclear deterrent due to some lack of confidence in the United States. There were, surprisingly, no recommendations to the effect that, since one or another balance was shifting in favor of the Soviets, France/ Western Europe should move to build up political fences with them. Indeed, recommendations that the United States or Western countries as a group increase their flexible-response capabilities signified willingness to continue working within the American-Western alliance context. Whether the decreasing number of flexible-response recommendations over time signified decreasing willingness to do so is a question worthy of investigation in future research.

SUMMARY OF SIGNIFICANT FINDINGS

Some of the more significant findings of this research are as follows:

The strategic nuclear balance by far was the subject of the greatest number of balance comparisons while the overall U. S. -USSR air and conventional or ground forces balances elicited the fewest assessments.

DN authors making comparisons tended to view the conventional or ground forces balance much more in NATO-Soviet Union/Soviet bloc terms (N/W-S/S) than in U. S. -USSR terms. The opposite was true for the naval balance.

Discounting the overall air balance, the United States consistently dominated—both over the long-term and in recent years—in the areas of strategic bombs and warheads, ballistic-missile submarines, and strategic aviation. There was no comparable area for the Soviets if one discounts the conventional-or-ground-forces balance due to the small number of comparisons. (See, however, footnote on page 130.)

The superpowers were generally viewed as equal in the strategic-nuclear balance over the long term with this trend becoming overwhelming in the last years of the study.

When shifts in the balances did occur as a result of comparing the last two five-year periods, they did not favor the United States. Both the strategic-missile and naval balances shifted from U. S. dominance toward equality.

Some balance areas (particularly strategic bombs and warheads, naval, and strategic aviation) elicited a greater tendency among DN

authors to think of them in quantitative terms than did others—
particularly the strategic-nuclear and the conventional-or-ground-
forces balances. The data, however, are limited for this last area.

The U. S. Government (especially the Defense Department)
was most often acknowledged as the source of information concerning
the capabilities being compared, followed by annuals specializing in
national military-force levels. The London International Institute for
Strategic Studies also figured prominently as an organizational
source. At no time did any author indicate use of Soviet information.

Three recommendations recurred most frequently, very often
in conjunction with viewing the strategic-nuclear balance as equal.
These encouraged development of a force de frappe by France or
Western Europe, an increase in flexible-response capabilities on the
part of the West or the United States, and implementation of a
Western program in the late 1950s and early 1960s to counter Soviet
politicopsychological advances in the Third World.

Contrary to this writer's expectations, there were few recommendations supporting strategic-arms limitations: no recommendations calling for mutual, balanced conventional-force reductions; no
recommendations that the United States increase its strategic-
missile arsenal as that balance shifted markedly toward equality
in the 1970s; only one recommendation encouraging France to develop
her own conventional-force capabilities; and no recommendations
calling upon France or Western Europe to build up political fences
with the Soviets as balances shifted away from the United States.

NOTES

1. See Donald C. Daniel, DÉFENSE NATIONALE Perceptions
of the US–Soviet Military Balances, Naval Postgraduate School
Technical Report 56D176111, (Monterey, Calif.: November, 1976).

2. The strategic-nuclear balance category includes all comparisons of U. S. and Soviet capabilities to win a nuclear exchange
and/or inflict nuclear destruction. It also encompasses references
restricted to comparing overall strategic-nuclear delivery capabilities.
It does not include references concerned with comparing more
specific capabilities such as strategic missile systems per se or
nuclear bombs. These are dealt with under other categories.

3. This category includes references comparing which side
had more and/or better bombs and warheads, more associated
megatonnage, or better bomb- and warhead-development programs.
Some comparisons dealt only with bombs or only with warheads
while others dealt with both as a group and were so coded. In most
cases, identifying comparisons for coding was a relatively simple task,

but there was difficulty in ascertaining if megatonnage comparisons dealt with total megatonnage or with warhead megatonnage only. This writer did not control for the difference.

4. The "strategic missiles (aggregate)" heading encompasses references to strategic missiles-in-general, land-based ICBMs, and SLBMs. Comparisons were readily identifiable and dealt either with which side had more and/or better missiles or better associated development programs. If a reference to strategic missiles-in-general was accompanied by clearly differentiated comparison of land-based ICBM's or SLBM's, then the ICBM or SLBM reference was coded also.

5. This balance includes all statements as to which side had more and/or better boats and all statements comparing the progress each side was making in its boat development and production programs.

6. Included in this category are references comparing which side had more and/or better bombers in general (more and/or better strategic bombers in particular), better-strategic aviation capability, or a better bomber or strategic-aviation development program. Of primary concern were references to heavy or long-range bombers or bombers which could leave one side's homeland, strike the other's, and return. No attempt was made to control whether a DN author's reference to "strategic bombers," or "bombers" in general, was meant to include medium bombers, light bombers, or forward-based tactical aircraft.

7. This category aggregates together references to the general or overall conventional-forces balance and to the general or overall ground-forces balance. They were aggregated because some authors clearly referred to one or the other's superiority in "conventional," "classical," or "traditional" forces but then restricted discussion to ground forces. Comparisons of overall conventional naval or air power are dealt with in other categories.

8. This category includes all statements focusing on which navy is superior overall as well as all references restricted to comparing which had more ships or tonnage, technically better ships, or better ship-development programs.

9. Coded under this category were statements to the effect that one or the other side had more air power, more and/or better aircraft over-all, or a better aircraft-development program.

8

JAPANESE ELITE ASSESSMENTS OF THE REGIONAL SUPERPOWER MILITARY BALANCE

Paul Langer

INTRODUCTION

No systematic study of the Japanese elite's perceptions of the U. S. -USSR military balance is known to exist. On the other hand, we do have substantial documentary and a good deal of impressionistic information on this question. An analysis of the available data thus can provide a general idea of the Japanese leadership's interpretation of world events and of its assessment of the international balance of forces.

In focusing on the views of the Japanese elite rather than on those of the Japanese public (as USIA surveys do), the problem posed itself of defining which individuals and interest groups should be considered to make up Japan's elite. For the purposes of this study, the criterion guiding this determination has been to include those individuals, organizations, or interest groups which either participate directly in the process of making Japan's policies or, by virtue of their social, economic, or political position or their special expertise, have important influence on those who do make policy. In practice, this meant an exploration of (1) the views and perspectives of Japanese political and government leaders and those in policy-making positions within the powerful Japanese bureaucracy; (2) the opinions held by Japan's business world—as reflected, for example, by the highly influential Keidanren (Federation of Economic Organizations) and its subsections; and (3) the views of those advisers, commentators, and defense, foreign-policy-and technology experts who are known to play a role in the Japanese decision-making process in foreign and national-security policy through their influence on the policy-making elite. This categorization reflects not only the writer's analysis

of Japan's power structure, but is shared by most experts on
Japan.

The opinions of individuals in the above categories were gleaned
from a variety of sources: official and unofficial documents, speeches,
policy statements, and writings; conference proceedings and other
reports by third parties—Japanese and U. S. , and personal interviews
with representative Japanese figures whom the writer has known for
some time. While use was made of the information accumulated over
many years during the writer's frequent trips to Japan, most of the
interviews took place during 1974 and 1975, either in Japan or in the
United States, and arose from opportunities created by research on
other facets of the U. S. -Japanese relationship. Since most individuals
interviewed preferred not to have their views attributed to them in
writing, no reference to their identity is made in the text.

JAPANESE PERSPECTIVES ON THE OUTSIDE WORLD

Insularity and Weak Threat-Perceptions

Ever since Japan regained its sovereignty some two decades
ago, the ruling conservatives and the opposition have been arguing
over Japan's international alignment and the most effective way of
assuring the nation's security. The existence of such divergent views
imposes severe constraints on Japan's defense strategy and dis-
courages the Japanese government from playing an activist role in
international affairs. [1] Yet, a closer examination of the Japanese
scene suggests that, despite these differences, most Japanese,
including the leadership, share certain basic perspectives on the
outside world—perspectives which stand in marked contrast to those
of the European allies of the United States. These Japanese international perspectives can be summarized under two headings:
insularity and weak threat-perception.

The Japanese themselves are deeply conscious of the insular
mental attitudes (shimaguni konjo) which mark their relationship to
the outside world and tend to set them apart from it. But noting the
rapid pace of the Western-style modernization of Japanese daily life
and the Japanese economy's ever-growing global involvement, one
might be tempted to play down this characteristic as diminishing in
relevance for the Japanese international outlook. Nothing could be
farther from the truth. Language and cultural-psychological barriers
continue to present enormous obstacles to international communications
with Japan. At the same time that the Japanese are economically
more deeply involved with other nations than ever before, they remain,
to a considerable degree, isolated from the Western developed nations

with its own very distinctive value system and perspectives. Para-
doxically, although the Japanese have developed one of the world's
most highly developed international communications networds, in
their perceptions they continue to remain remote from developments
abroad and admit to a lack of "feel" for them. (The extremely homogeneous ethnic and cultural make-up of the Japanese population may
account as much for this national insularity as does the country's
island location off the Asian continent.)

These observations apply, if to a lesser degree, to the policy-
making elite as they do to the general public. At the top of the
Japanese power pyramid stand men who are singularly Japanese in
their social and psychological outlook, personal associations, and
world-view. Japan's decision makers in the political, economic, and
bureaucratic spheres tend to have only a superficial intellectual
involvement with the world beyond Japan. Hence the significance in
Japan of such intermediaries as the "defense intellectuals" and other
specialists in international affairs who can serve as interpreters of
international developments for an audience of policy makers not well
equipped intellectually to read the news from abroad.

The insularity of Japan also contributes to the weak external-
threat perceptions that characterize Japan and stand in sharp contrast
to European reactions. With the exception of the Allied (that is,
U. S.) occupation after World War II, the Japanese islands have
never experienced foreign military incursions. Whenever Japan has
been entangled in military ventures, it has been the result of Japanese
initiatives and has occurred away from the home islands. If anything,
Japan's defeat in the war has reduced the Japanese people's concern
with an external threat, as Japan's security is being assured by the
American military presence and formal U. S. defense guarantees.
So long as the United States is acknowledged to be the world's
paramount power, the Japanese—further protected by their physical
distance from potential adversaries—can feel secure and free to focus
their energies on domestic construction. In the past three decades,
this inward-directed effort has minimized Japan's involvement in
international affairs and, thereby also, the Japanese people's exposure
to external problems.

Another factor deserves mention in this context. Japan's disarmament after the war, its rejection of military power as an instrument
of national policy (Article 9 of the Japanese postwar constitution),
and the Japanese leaders' conscious decision to build economic
rather than military strength have naturally tended to divert their
attention away from global military concerns. Nations, like
individuals, presumably are inclined to see the world in an image
fitting their preferred strategies. Rightly or wrongly, therefore—
and we are not concerned here with judging the validity of Japanese

views but with describing them—the Japanese have commonly viewed military power as of less utility in assuring their national security than the protection provided by economic strength and world-wide trade relations. The conviction is by now deeply embedded in the minds of the Japanese people—and not only of the general public— that so long as Japan continues its present policies, there is no good reason, or incentive,for the Soviet Union or any other nation to threaten the security of Japan.

Reinforcing these conclusions are certain widely-held notions about the U. S. -USSR military relationship. In the past, statements by authoritative Japanese (for example, the Defense Agency Chief and Japan's Foreign Minister) confirm that from the Japanese leadership's viewpoint the U. S. -USSR equilibrium has positive global significance in the sense that it renders an armed clash of the superpowers highly unlikely and thereby also sets natural limits to the localized conflicts expected to occur from time to time on the fringes of the two competing alliance systems. In the Japanese view, there is no reason why any nation should wish to engage in aggression against a virtually unarmed Japan, allied to the United States and deeply enmeshed in mutually beneficial economic exchanges with the world's major nations, although there remains some fear that Japan might be drawn into a local conflict. Thus, under present conditions, characterized by the absence of acute tension in Japan's international environment, one finds little concern among the Japanese leadership about serious repercussions for Japan resulting in the short term from the U. S. -USSR global military competition. *

There is another difference between Japanese international perspectives and those of the European noncommunist nations. In Europe, one notes a strong conviction that the U. S. -USSR global balance has a direct and immediate bearing on the security of every European nation and that Soviet challenges, wherever they may occur in Europe, are viewed as interrelated and affecting all of Europe. Hence the deeply felt need for a united front against Soviet pressures. The Japanese, on the other hand, view their security as being assured and essentially distinct from that of most of Asia. They see the rest of Asia in a state of extreme flux, where the threats to

---

*Japanese opinion makers and defense intellectuals participating in Moscow in late 1974 in a conference devoted to an appraisal of Soviet-Japanese relations saw such convictions confirmed when their Soviet counterparts reportedly downplayed the U. S. -Japanese security pact as being no more than one element in U. S. attempts to maintain a U. S. -USSR global balance rather than being specifically aimed at the Soviet Union.

stability tend to be multiple and largely internal rather than single, external, and easily defined. In line with these basic perceptions, the Japanese elite recognized no place in the Far East for a strong and broad military alliance that would include Japan.

It is understandable, then, that the Japanese leadership has been much less preoccupied with global noneconomic concerns and the U.S. and Soviet military roles than is the case with the Europeans. The relative intensity of Japanese sensitivities can best be depicted with concentric circles: at the center is, of course, the preoccupation of the leadership with the state of affairs at home; then, concerns about the security of the area around Japan and Korea; further out, a continued strong interest in the stability of conditions along the arc from Northeast to Southeast Asia; and, finally, a broad, general, but rather remote, concern with the state of the global U.S.-USSR military balance. Although this balance is acknowledged to have its indirect effect on areas of special interest to Japan, it is viewed as a problem quite beyond Japan's ability to affect. In that sense, the Japanese persepctive is that of a regional and economic, rather than that of a world, power.

Japanese Preferences Vis-à-vis the Superpowers

Perceptions of reality filter through the prism of policy preferences. What, then, are Japanese psychological predispositions and preferences with regard to the United States and the Soviet Union? The answers are not difficult to ascertain. They are reflected in everything we know about Japanese views of each country, in Japanese behavior toward the two big powers, in Japanese writings and official statements, and in the many public opinion polls conducted on the subject over the years.

It seems hardly necessary to go into detail regarding Japanese attitudes toward the United States—a subject on which much has been written on both sides of the Pacific. While there have been ups and downs in the U.S.-Japanese relationship since the war, and while the relationship has never been completely free of friction, Japanese attitudes toward the United States remain essentially positive, despite (or perhaps because of?) the wartime defeat and the effects of the postwar military occupation of Japan. This is a tribute to U.S. policy and to the success of the economic, social, and political restructuring of postwar Japan in which the United States played, initially at least, a dominant role. It is also an indication that the Japanese leadership sees Japan's national interest in close political and military bonds with the United States rather than in a neutralist or unaligned posture.

While the alliance rests primarily on economic, and thus perhaps shallow, foundations rather than on a consciousness of shared values, this has never really subtracted from the essentially positive Japanese perception of the United States. These positive sentiments are held not only by the vast majority of the general public as well as by Japan's conservative leadership, but they also are present as a latent force far into the liberal and left wings of Japanese opposition politics. After more than two decades of close political, economic, and military ties between the two countries, the alliance with the United States has proved its worth to most Japanese—even to many in the political opposition, as is evidenced in its leaders' increasingly gingerly handling of the security-pact issue. So long as Japan prefers to assure its security through a military alliance, the United States remains the logical and favored partner in the eyes of the majority of the Japanese people and its leadership. In their view, U. S. policy objectives and world outlook continue to be essentially compatible with the perceived national interest of postwar Japan.

In studying one nation's response to another nation, one encounters a composite of predispositions, assumptions, and reactions. The resulting image plays a very real role in influencing a nation's international behavior and its foreign-policy choices. Such an image appears to be primarily the result of the cumulative effect of the historical experience. It encompasses conflicts and alliances— military, political, and ideological. It is affected by geographic and economic factors, by the scope, depth, and nature of cultural inter- change, by the intensity of the flow of communications between the countries concerned, and by the actions and interpersonal relation- ships of their leaders.

It has already been pointed out that the Japanese image of the United States is on balance a very favorable one. Japanese perspec- tives on the Soviet Union, on the other hand, are strongly and nega- tively marked by past confrontations of a military and ideological nature. World War II further accentuated Japanese feelings of hostility and distrust when Soviet forces suddenly attacked in Manchuria during the last days of the fighting (despite the still valid nonaggression pact with Japan), subsequently held a million or more Japanese military and civilians in camps (where many of them did not survive the rigorous conditions), and seized territory traditionally considered Japanese. Thereafter, Soviet international behavior—in Eastern Europe and closer to Japan—coupled with the rapid buildup of military strength, did nothing to improve the Soviet reputation in Japan. Moreover, in the competition with China for Japanese support, the Soviet Union from the beginning was handicapped. Chinese propaganda in Japan still further blackened the Soviet image. During the past decade, Soviet approaches to Japan and expanding economic exchanges have provided a somewhat better environment for Soviet-Japanese relations. Nevertheless, Japanese distrust of the Soviet Union remains deep-rooted among the elite, especially among the older generation which provides Japan's political leadership. On public opinion polls, the Soviet Union continues to vie with the two Koreas for the spot of "most disliked nation" in Japan. In the USSR's global competition with the United States, Japanese sympathies and Japan's national interest are acknowledged to be on the U.S. side. The Japanese leaders realistically view the Soviet Union as a power to be reckoned with. They view it as a potentially troublesome neighbor with whom relations should be improved, but who also deserves to be watched with suspicion.

Reliance on U.S. Information

The nature and dimensions of the channels through which one nation learns about another obviously exert an important influence on the perceptions of one nation by another. The flow of information entering Japan from the United States has always been vastly superior in quantity, quality, and diversity from that coming out of the Soviet Union. There is no precise way of comparing the two information flows, but a ratio of 100:1 is probably not an exaggeration. Certainly, both the Japanese general public and the elite are notably more familiar with all aspects of American conditions and policies than with those of the Soviet Union. The reasons lie in the different natures of the two societies as well as in the very extensive and still progressing enmeshing of Japanese and American societies. In contrast to the trickle of Japanese visitors to the Soviet Union going there for political, commercial, or cultural purposes, and to the even fewer Soviets coming to Japan, millions of Americans have had direct contact with the Japanese since the days of the military occupation and hundreds of thousands of Japanese have visited or lived in the United States as tourists, students, business people, technicians, and scientists. Every day the average Japanese is exposed to the English language—in school, on television and radio, in advertisements, in the press, and in literature. Familiarity with the Russian language remains the exception in Japan, being found primarily among students of literature or among government research analysts—concentrated in the Foreign Ministry, the Defense Agency, and the several organizations concerned with foreign intelligence. Not surprisingly, these analysts are severely handicapped by the less accessible nature of Soviet society and the consequent paucity of data on Soviet developments. This applies particularly to information which would allow continuous, direct monitoring of Soviet military strength. Thus,

today the flow of information about Soviet developments, especially
with regard to military matters, enters Japan almost entirely by way
of the United States rather than from the Soviet Union.

Japanese perceptions of relative U. S. and Soviet strengths
thus tend to be powerfully influenced by U. S. views, perspectives,
and judgments. This phenomenon is accentuated by the large gap
between the levels of U. S. and Japanese sophistication in the understanding of advanced-weapons technology and the complexities of
nuclear strategy. Virtually all nonactive Japanese military experts
and defense intellectuals have been trained in the United States or
else have honed their analytic skills through frequent contacts with
their U. S. counterparts and through their reading of the pertinent
U. S. literature. Much of the Japanese perspective on the world-wide
military balance and the relative strengths and weaknesses of the
two superpowers is thus the result of continuous exposure to U. S.
views and interpretations.

Available evidence indicates that virtually all U. S. public
information of importance and relevant to the state of the U. S.-USSR
military competition reaches Japan sooner or later through one or
another of the many existing channels. Conversations in Tokyo,
confirmed by a review of the pertinent Japanese literature, suggest
that in this massive flow of information certain sources exert a
particularly strong influence on the Japanese elite's views and that
the number of these sources is quite limited. Among them are, not
surprisingly, statements by the U. S. Secretaries of Defense and
State, the military service chiefs, and high officers in the Pacific
command. (To a lesser extent, this is true also of the statements of
their Soviet counterparts.) Thus, the annual posture statement of the
Defense department and its State Department version are paid special
attention by Japanese officials* and experts who brief their superiors
or comment on the trend of world developments, although the political
element in such statements is recognized. To the extent that budget
figures allow a detailed analysis of U. S. military programs and their
evolution, the annual U. S. defense budget is also examined with much
interest in Japan. Such documents are usually compared with the
versions of earlier years in order to detect trends and new developments in U. S. military estimates and strategies. Presidential
speeches, interviews, and messages are given attention primarily for
indications of the future direction of U. S. policy rather than for their

----

*Hence, in evaluating the military strength of the nations
relevant to the security of Japan, the recent White Papers (1976 and
1977) issued by Japan's Defense Agency rely heavily on such official
U. S. assessments.

value as sources of specific information. Thus, a speech delivered
in Kansas City in July 1971 by President Nixon—and largely ignored
by the U. S. public—was studied in Japan for clues as to the meaning
for Japan of the Nixon doctrine which long puzzled the Japanese as to
its concrete implications. It is not always realized in the U. S. how
carefully Congressional debates, testimony, and reports are
scrutinized in Japan for information which may elucidate and comple-
ment (or contradict) the data provided to the Japanese government
in official U. S. communications (including those submitted by the
U. S. side in connection with the various regularly scheduled bilateral
talks or the exchange of intelligence information). The very diversity
of views and arguments expressed in the Congressional forum enriches—
and often confuses—Japanese interpretations of U. S. thinking.

A similar and very important role is played by the many
nonofficial studies and analyses prepared by a number of U. S. and
other research organizations or individual specialists on strategic
problems enjoying a high reputation in Japan. Much of the Japanese
elite's thinking about the U. S. -USSR balance turns out to be inspired
by the International Institute of Strategic Studies' Military Balance
or such reference works as Jane's Fighting Ships, Jane's All the
World's Aircraft, the SIPRI Yearbooks, the Brookings Institution's
Setting National Priorities (and related studies), and many analytical
reports issued by The RAND Corporation and several other U. S.
research organizations concerned with problems of national security
and weapons technology. Nor should one underestimate the role
played by a handful of U. S. and other prestigious newspapers and
periodicals in shaping the Japanese elite's views. Traditionally,
the New York Times has occupied a special place on this short list
which includes a few quality non-U. S. papers like the Times of London
and Le Monde. Pravda and Izvestia, although actually read by a small
number of Japanese specialists, nevertheless in their translated
form constitute important sources of information, as do the more
specialized Soviet publications dealing with military matters and
world affairs. In sum, the Japanese elite obtain their information on
the state of the U. S. -USSR competition very much as do their U. S.
counterparts. It is only natural therefore that Japanese elite perceptions in that regard often parallel U. S. views.

The influence of the personal factor in shaping Japanese perspectives is a considerable one. The major reasons for this have
already been referred to but bear repetition: the fact that Japan is a
society in which interpersonal relations are particularly important;
conditions under which Japan today largely lacks the information,
sophistication, and experience to evaluate many of the specific
technical aspects of the U. S. -USSR military competition; the heavy
reliance on U. S. military power reflected in intensive interaction

between the two military establishments; the limited number of Japanese individuals engaged in, and thus competent to judge, issues of military strategy and their consequent heavy reliance on information provided by U. S. sources and contacts; and the intensive U. S. - Japanese dialogue conducted between the two countries' political, economic, scientific, and cultural elites as well as between their militaries.

Official exchanges of views between U. S. and Japanese government leaders—civilian and military—exert a demonstrable influence on the views of the Japanese decision makers insofar as the appraisal of the U. S. -USSR balance is concerned, as the U. S. side is assumed to have a virtual monopoly on inside technical knowledge and sophisticated analytic capability. This has been shown repeatedly in such matters as the Japanese assessment of the significance of new weapons developments like the ABM, or MIRV. Much U. S. influence is also exerted through informal U. S. -Japanese contacts involving private citizens—a condition almost totally absent from Soviet-Japanese relations. Although the Soviet Union has belatedly begun to make efforts to institute a dialogue with Japanese opinion leaders and decision makers, this attempt is still in its early stages and is hampered by institutional, political, and psychological barriers between the two societies. On the other hand, the U. S. -Japanese military alliance and its ramifications—exchanges of personnel, training programs, licensing and joint weapons production, and the like—provide the Japanese side with a continuous opportunity to gauge and be influenced by American perspectives. In recent years, hardly a month has gone by in which prominent and influential Americans and Japanese have not met somewhere to discuss international issues at conferences, seminars, or workshops. In many instances, it is possible to trace back to such meetings the emergence of specific Japanese views on issues pertinent to an evaluation of the U. S. -USSR military balance.

In sum, all available evidence suggests the key role of the United States in forming Japanese perceptions of the outside world, especially where judgments of a military or technological nature are concerned. Nevertheless, differences in world-outlook, priorities, and policy context do not make Japanese perspectives simple mirror images of American views. In the following, an attempt will be made to provide an admittedly cursory and tentative exposition of some of the more interesting Japanese perceptions regarding major aspects of the current state of U. S. -USSR competition. These observations represent a distillate of information gained from the writer's frequent personal contacts with relevant Japanese and from a continuing examination of the pertinent Japanese literature of the past two years.

SOME JAPANESE ELITE PERCEPTIONS

Japanese elite perceptions of the U. S. -USSR military balance are a composite of diverse considerations. Of course, genuinely military judgments enter importantly into the assessment. So do political, economic, and technological assessments of observable developments and trends produced by the interplay of the two big powers. But the resulting conclusions regarding the state of the U. S. - USSR balance are also functions of a much broader set of considerations related to the prevailing psychological climate in Japan, the nation's priorities as perceived by its leaders, as well as national reactions to the behavior of the two superpowers—factors that have been discussed earlier.

Thus, judgments on the part of Japan's power elite as to "who is ahead" or "who is advancing and who is retreating" are not the product of a single assessment—military, technological, economic, or political—but the result of a combination of considerations, the elements of which are not always analytically separable. Nevertheless, it is generally possible to determine at least what kinds of international events and developments, or actions taken by the United States or the Soviet Union, have markedly affected Japanese elite perceptions of the U. S. -USSR military balance and how and why any of their previously held views have been modified.

The question may legitimately be raised whether it is possible at all to generalize about the Japanese elite's perceptions of the U. S. - USSR balance since in Japan, as in other democratic societies, the elite can presumably not be precisely defined and since, at any rate, it may be expected to hold a spectrum of views on the subject. In answer to this question, it should be pointed out that this analysis consciously confines the inquiry to those Japanese circles making up the country's power elite and to those who by virtue of their professional functions have direct influence on it. The scope of this study thus does not encompass the views of Japan's socialist or communist opposition leaders who do not directly participate in determining Japan's foreign alignment or defense orientation. Nor does it purport to reflect the judgments of antiestablishment activists and ideologically oriented intellectuals associated with the left wing of Japanese politics. The principal components of Japan's power elite—the government bureaucracy, the ruling conservative political party, the leaders of finance and business, and those professionals who as experts, advisers, and commentators have a continuing impact on the views of Japan's leadership—are quite homogeneous, sharing a common value system and basic perspectives. Differences in these leaders' assessments of the U. S. -USSR military balance tend to be, rather than fundamental disagreements, differences of emphasis and degree originating, for the most part, in their differing professional vantage points and areas of responsibility.

What, then, is the prevailing view among the Japanese elite regarding the present correlation of U. S. and Soviet forces operating on the world scene, and what changes, if any, do they expect in that regard in the decades ahead? In a broad and undifferentiated way, they judge the United States and the Soviet Union to have reached a state of "near-parity" because the United States is believed to retain some degree of superiority in the purely technical aspects of military power; but this U. S. edge is thought to be rapidly diminishing to the point that strategically it may no longer count for much. In essence, this state of near-parity is seen as producing relatively stable international relations, for, like powerful sumo wrestlers (an image frequently used to describe the situation), the superpowers are straining to upset each other while being locked in a grip that virtually immobilizes them. Hence, for the time being at least, the United States and the Soviet Union are forced to concede strategic parity to each other. At the same time, their strengths are such that no third power is now, or will be in the foreseeable future, even remotely in a position to challenge the two superpowers militarily. In the Japanese view, these circumstances create conditions conducive to a continuing detente in superpower relationships. In turn, this state of affairs is also considered highly desirable from the point of view of Japan's national interest since the resulting relaxation of tensions not only prevents a catastrophic clash of the two big powers and their allies, but imposes limits on the scope and violence of local military conflicts that, even in an era of detente, might occur from time to time on the fringes of the two alliance systems.

If the prevailing Japanese view of the U. S. -USSR balance shows a lack of serious immediate concern about the implications for Japan of the present state of U. S. -USSR strategic relations, this does not necessarily hold true of Japanese assessments of future developments. It is widely believed that the long-term trend of U. S. -USSR strategic power ratios may hold danger for the status quo, for SALT and other U. S. -USSR arms agreements are not interpreted as evidence that the Soviets have abandoned ambitions to achieve military superiority over the United States. While it is acknowledged that many things can change between now and the late 1980s, trends in the balance of forces are on the whole perceived, over the longer run, as tending to favor the Soviet Union.

What are the reasons for such Japanese views about possible changes in the future U. S. -USSR balance? The answer is evident from Japanese comments on the world situation including those expressed in private by members of the elite. The Japanese are simply extending into the future the trend of world affairs of the last

decade as they see it. They see no reason to modify significantly such
a projection. The United States is judged to have had absolute superiority in all major areas of national power perhaps as late as the
1950s. Since then, the world has witnessed a relative decline in U. S.
influence, the devolution of U. S. international commitments and
responsibilities (the Nixon doctrine is generally referred to as one
of the important symptoms of this development), the Soviet attainment
of military parity or near-parity with the United States, the gradual
narrowing of the existing technological gap between the two powers at
least insofar as military capabilities are concerned, the well-
advertised domestic (socioeconomic and political) difficulties the
United States has been experiencing in the past years, and a number
of what are deemed to have been American failures in international
affairs—prominently among them, the Indochina conflict and
occasionally also the India-Pakistan War and the situation in Africa.
The United States has been unable to stem the gradual intrusion of
Soviet power into regions which once were closed to it. It is acknowledged that to extrapolate from such trends may be misleading as
trends are reversible. Yet, it is seen as a fact that the Soviet Union
has advanced in a very short span of time from a state of clear
strategic inferiority to one approaching parity; that it has become
a factor, politically and militarily, in an ever-widening portion of the
world. It is not so much the existing correlation of military forces that
gives rise to concern, but the momentum which appears to carry the
Soviet position forward. Will this momentum continue unabated during
the next decade and, if so, what will be the results for world stability?
These are the questions being asked in Japan, not insistently as yet,
but occasionally and with some hesitation.

Specific developments or events which have given rise to such
interpretations can be arranged under four categories, only two of
which are of a genuinely military nature. In the first place, there is
the question of superiority in sophisticated nuclear weaponry. The
Japanese leadership continues to have great confidence in U. S. technological capacities. At the same time, the impression has gained
ground—strongly supported by U. S. analyses circulating in Japan—
that, at least in the field of military applications, the gap has been
steadily narrowing. This process has been observed in Soviet
nuclear-weapons development from its inception. The latest example,
frequently mentioned in Japan, is the issue of MIRVs. Rightly or
wrongly, the Soviet Union is believed to have progressed in this field
much more rapidly than had been anticipated in U. S. estimates, so
that agreements concluded in Moscow (SALT I) and believed to have
been premised on a slower Soviet rate of MIRV development may give
some advantage to the Soviet Union. The United States is conceded
superiority in tactical nuclear weapons, but, in regard to strategic-

nuclear weaponry, the equilibrium is now considered a more pre-
carious one. Japanese strategic analysts recognize that the superior
throw-weight of Soviet missiles may be a reflection of inferior Soviet
technical capability to produce more accurate weaponry, but it is
also argued that the very massiveness of the Soviet weapons could
have a psychological and political effect and, more importantly, that
the Soviet Union in seeking to give these large weapons greater
accuracy could gain a further advantage in the future. Arms-control
agreements may have the effect of pushing the military competition
in the direction of qualitative, rather than of quantitative, improvements of weaponry, conditions which traditionally would favor the
United States, but the rapid rate of Soviet advances in military
technology is beginning, at least in the view of some influential
Japanese, to cast doubt on this assumption.

The second area of U. S. -USSR competition, that of conventional
forces, is providing even more food for thought. It is not just the
force ratios which are shifting to the advantage of the Soviet Union,
but a major Soviet effort is successfully being made to remedy
existing deficiencies. This is seen with regard to Soviet aviation
(where the MiG-25 is reported to have performed very well in the
Middle East), but more conspicuously with regard to Soviet naval
forces. Japan being an island nation with a navy tradition, and in
view of the important role assigned to the U. S. Seventh Fleet in
Japanese thinking with regard to maintaining stability in the Pacific,
it is not surprising that the issue of the steady growth and geographic
advance of Soviet naval forces is prominently mentioned by Japanese
leaders and commentators as dangerously increasing Soviet military
capabilities and political leverage far beyond the Soviet defense
perimeter. Comments on the Soviet tonnage increase, and the
qualitative improvement of the Soviet naval forces, tend to be
juxtaposed with statements about the declining number of U. S. naval
craft and their growing age. A prominent U. S. admiral's warning
that the Pacific has ceased to be an American lake was widely taken
up in Japan. In that context, the Soviet naval exercises termed OKEAN
II, conducted in 1975, have had a particularly strong effect on
Japanese analyses of military and foreign policy issues; analysts of
the exercise have dwelled at some length on the greater dimensions
and ambitiousness of the 1975 operation compared to its 1970
predecessor.

In a similar vein, one encounters comments about the lengthening
reach of Soviet intervention abroad. (It is this third area of arguments
pointing toward an increasing Soviet political world role at the expense
of the United States that is particularly effective with the general
public.) There is, of course, the case of Soviet influence in the
Indochina war which is believed to have resulted in a strengthening

of the Soviet position in the Pacific region; India, where a formalized rapprochement (now questionable) with the Soviet Union could open up a vast subcontinent and adjacent seas to Soviet influence; Africa and the Middle East, where instability and uncertainty continue to characterize the situation, but where the United States is seen as conceding a role to the Soviet Union in a region from which the Soviets' influence had hitherto been barred.

But Japanese doubts about the continued ability of the United States to prevail over the Soviet Union appear to be less rooted in the actual and concrete manifestations of expanding Soviet power than in vague doubts about U. S. will and determination to maintain the U. S. world role, to stand up to Soviet pressures, and to bear the attendant economic and psychological cost. Much of what has taken place in the world at large, as well as in the United States since the days of the Cuban missile crisis, seems to be feeding Japanese doubts. As with other Japanese perceptions about the state of the U. S.–USSR balance, Japanese conclusions regarding a weakening of the United States appear to originate from U. S. analyses and declarations rather than from independent Japanese judgments.

It would be an exaggeration to say that the Japanese elite feels anxiety over the future of the U. S.–USSR balance. That is not the case. For the moment, Japan feels relatively secure in conditions of U. S.–USSR strategic parity and expects this state to endure at least for the near future. Further, it is a common assumption in Japan that, so long as the United States will compete for world influence with the USSR, the U. S. nuclear umbrella over Japan will not be withdrawn and aggression against Japan will thus be deterred. In these circumstances, the Japanese leadership sees no reason for immediate concern about possible Soviet actions directed against Japan. This has been evidenced time and again, most recently when Foreign Minister Gromyko ended his unsuccessful mission to Tokyo (January 1976) with parting words that could be interpreted as an implicit warning to the Japanese government. Nor do occasional Soviet incursions into Japanese air and sea space cause great excitement in Japan. In summing up the situation, it would be fair to say that the Japanese elite's perceptions about the global U. S.–USSR military balance reveal at this point merely the existence of a mild degree of uneasiness about that balance's future evolution.

If the global balance of forces is judged to be as yet no cause for immediate concern, it is also perhaps because it is perceived as a remote issue over which Japan has at any rate little influence. This is demonstrated by Japanese reactions to SALT and other arms-control agreements, either concluded or under discussion between the United States and the USSR. SALT has not aroused much interest in Japan. Only specialists have examined the substantive issues involved, pointing, among other things, to the possible relevance of future SALT agreements to the defense of Japan insofar as questions of range limitations for offensive weapons are concerned. Generally, SALT has been interpreted in Japan as an understanding between the two superpowers to promote certain coinciding interests and only symbolically as a move toward disarmament or as evidence of an approaching end of the race for arms superiority. The issues involved in the SALT talks are viewed essentially as global and as transcending the range of Japanese interests. Moreover, they are not well under-stood in Japan in their technical implications except by a few specialists. Their conclusions, in turn, tend to be based on U. S. analyses and on discussions with their American counterparts. Thus, to the extent that any critical comments are made about the SALT talks, they repeat American warnings against harboring illusions about Soviet intentions and Soviet willingness to live up to arms agreements. Such warnings strike a sympathetic chord among many Japanese in view of Japan's past bitter experiences with the Russians.

The region around Japan is very much in a state of flux providing incentives for the superpowers as well as for China to com-pete and expand their influence. Hence, American and Soviet behavior and, more specifically, their force deployments and demonstrations are watched in Japan as indicators of future trends.

In that context, OKEAN II and the steady growth and increasing visibility of the Soviet naval forces in the Pacific and Indian Oceans are read as reflections of Soviet ambitions. Similarly, U. S. deploy-ments and the extent to which the once predominant American role is being maintained in the region are interpreted not only as directly relevant to the security of the area from Soviet pressures and in-fluence, but by implication also as measures of American will and determination in a world-wide frame. Thus, while U. S. pledges to continue to maintain forces and interest in Korea had an important positive effect on Japanese assessments, the U. S. plan to withdraw forces has again raised questions in the Japanese mind regarding U. S. intentions in the Pacific region.

SOME IMPLICATIONS

In conclusion, a few observations are in order regarding the implications of Japanese elite perceptions of the U. S. -USSR military balance. In the first place, the Japanese show little concern about the global aspects of the issue which to them is one involving essentially only the two major players. While their interest certainly lies in preventing this global balance from being destroyed, they feel impotent to do much to sustain it. They view the Soviet Union as having made great strides in recent years—militarily, technologically, and perhaps even politically (although clearly not economically)— toward superpower status rivaling that of the United States, which is seen as having meanwhile entered, temporarily perhaps, a period of relative decline. There remains in Japan strong confidence in U. S. technological superiority and in U. S. capacity to maintain the material foundations required for competition with the Soviet Union on at least equal terms. But one notes also some uneasiness about the future. That uneasiness stems from perceptions of weakening U. S. determination to carry on the competition, an aspect of power of which the Soviet Union is thought to have ample supplies. These perceptions may be responsible for a delicate change that has occurred in the thinking of what is still a minority among the Japanese elite with regard to the optimum way of ensuring Japan's national security. The need for maintaining the American alliance is acknowledged by them as strongly as ever. But one notes incipient support for the concept of supplementary security guarantees for Japan including Soviet participation in such an arrangement—a concept, incidentally, that in the past found advocates only among the opposition Socialists.

Evidence regarding the impact on Japanese perceptions of demonstrations of U. S. power through weapons demonstrations, space exploits, and other technical feats is contradictory. But Japanese assessments of U. S. strength are certainly affected in a significant way by the regional role of the United States in the Pacific. The importance of the Seventh Fleet as an indicator of American intentions has already been suggested. Its withdrawal or drastic reduction, if undertaken in a global context favorable to the Soviet Union, would likely be taken by the Japanese leadership as a significant signal that the regional balance was in the process of shifting due to declining U. S. determination. Such a development could prompt not only a reappraisal of Japanese conclusions regarding the state of the U. S.-USSR military balance, but consequences also could be felt in Japanese national-security policies. It could lead to a reopening of the internal debate regarding the limits of self-defense and the desirability of building indigenous deterrent power. In addition, one needs to emphasize once more the enormous influence of the U. S. self-view on Japanese perceptions of the U. S.-USSR balance: to what extent this balance appears to the Japanese elite to tilt in favor of the United States or the Soviet Union is, to a considerable extent, a function of the way the United States sees it and of how it communicates its views to the Japanese elite.

NOTES

1. For a detailed analysis of these issues, see the writer's Japanese National Security Policy—Domestic Determinants, R-1030-ISA (Santa Monica: The RAND Corporation, June 1972).

9

ARAB PERCEPTIONS OF THE REGIONAL SUPERPOWER MILITARY BALANCE

Ronald D. McLaurin

INTRODUCTION

Many argue that military force is too narrow a conceptual base for power status. It cannot be denied that mineral resources, productivity and productive capability, national character, and many other elements traditionally identified as ingredients in power ranking are relevant in influencing world affairs. Yet, ultimately, in the face of China's population, Japan's economic vitality, the mineral and other resources in many of the world's weakest states, and a poor correlation between geography and power status, perceived military capability seems still to equate more closely with power or influence. The Soviet Union is an excellent case in point. While it is not the economic or technological equal of the United States, most analysts have since World War II accepted that it and the United States together, being the world's military superpowers, dominate the international system.

One regional subsystem in which both the United States and the Soviet Union have important interests is the Middle East. Indeed,

We are deeply grateful for the conceptual assistance of Gerald Sullivan (then of the Defense Advanced Research Projects Agency) and our colleague, Paul A. Jureidini; for help by our colleagues Phillip P. Katz and Edward E. Azar (also with the University of North Carolina at Chapel Hill and the Center for Advanced Research, Chapel Hill, N. C.) in developing a codebook; and for the invaluable support of Suhaila Haddad (Library of Congress) and Edward Azar, respectively, in coding and analysis of the data.

the salience of superpower interests, investments, and commitment, combined with intraregional conflicts, have made this area the most explosive in the world. It is a region for which the superpowers have shown themselves willing to expend considerable resources—including potentially coercive resources such as military force—to influence the views of the local actors.

STUDY PURPOSE AND METHOD

The purpose of this study is to consider Arab perceptions of the Mideast superpower regional balance as these are reflected in Arab newspapers between 1965 and 1975. Two newspapers served as sources of data for the entire period with an additional two consulted when gathering data for 1975. The former are al-Ahram, a semiofficial Cairo daily, representing the Egyptian regime, and an-Nahar, the most important Beirut daily, highly regarded as independent in its editorial policies. The latter are al-Hayat, a Beirut daily representing the Saudi perspective, and ash-Sharq, a small daily, also published in Beirut but reflecting the Syrian viewpoint.

Content analysis was employed in order to gather data from these sources. It is a research method which aims at objective, quantitative, and systematic description of communications content. Although innumerable systems of content analysis vary markedly depending upon objectives, all must enable different coders to arrive at similar coding decisions on the same material, must organize content into discrete categories of which statistical analyses are possible, and must explicitly posit criteria for treatment of content. Detailed coding rules and procedures were developed and assembled together in what was termed the FACES codebook (i. e. , Codebook for the Force Assessment Content/Events Data System).[1] It is sufficient to say here that the unit of analysis was an article or article-segment discussing superpower military force events which occurred in or affected the areas from Morocco on the West to Iran on the east and from Turkey on the north to Oman on the south. These events included but were not limited to the conclusion of defense agreements; agreements on, implementation of, or other developments concerning arms transfers or arms control; weapons-systems developments and performance characteristics; advanced technology breakthroughs with potential military relevance; force deployments (including new weapons or additional manpower); the establishment, expansion, reduction, termination, or change in terms of reference of military missions in countries in or near the Middle East area; maneuvers and exercises; visits to these countries of armed forces, ships, aircraft, or personnel; military, including naval , operations in times of crisis; and policy decisions or statements by the executive or legislative branches relating to defense policy within the legislative branch.

Resources were inadequate for the systematic collection of data across one or more newspapers for the entire 1965-through-1975 time frame. Data gathering was restricted to those issues published during time periods when superpower military force events (such as those described above) either occurred in the Middle East or, if outside the area, were of such a magnitude that they might well be expected to influence regional perceptions. These were specifically selected with the intent that the various types of U.S.-USSR military force events should be represented, preferably by more than one example. Other than superpower ship visits, military maneuvers, exercises, and noncrisis deployments (mentioned nearly 290 times in the papers consulted), there were over 200 events (including crises and associated deployments) which guided the selection of dates with the majority occurring in 1970 and beyond. Obvious examples were the June War, the Yom Kippur War, the 1970 Jordanian crisis, and the Lebanese civil war. Others included the signing of the Nuclear Nonproliferation Treaty, the Czech invasion, the announcement of the Guam doctrine, the opening of SALT discussions, and the expulsion of Soviet advisers from Egypt.

DEVELOPMENT OF HYPOTHESES

A number of hypotheses were developed against which to test the data gathered. Their development and the order of their presentation reflect the categorization of superpower military force events contained in the FACES codebook. These hypotheses are as follows:

1. Symbolic force events in the Middle East are not related by the media to either the local superpower balance or to the superpowers' local capabilities.

2. U.S. weapons are generally considered superior in design and quality control to Soviet weapons of the same type. Exceptions are some SAM (surface-to-air missile) systems, ATGMs (antitank guided missiles), and the Kalashnikov AK-47 rifle. (These weapons were widely used by the Arabs and have been generally reported by the Western media to be highly regarded by the Arab forces using them.)

3. Foreign military missions are not considered as factors influencing either local superpower military capabilities or the regional balance between the United States and the USSR.

4. The Arab press does not relate weapons research and development (R&D) to the local military balance or to the local superpower military capabilities.

TABLE 9.1

Symbolic Force Events and the
Local Superpower Balance

Type of Event	Number of Obser- vations	Aggregate Space (cm^2)	Affecting Balance		Space	
			Obser- vations	Per- cent	(cm^2)	Per- cent
Visits	143	22,665	0	0	0	0
Games, maneuvers, exercises	40	2,401	0	0	0	0
Totals	183	25,066	0	0	0	0
Note: other deployments	155	15,547	2	1.3	686	4.1

Source: Compiled by author.

5. Arab media are not in a position to determine the time lag between research breakthrough and deployment. Consequently, these lags are not related by the Arab press to the local military balance between U.S. and Soviet forces.

6. On the other hand, deployments of new systems are seen by the media to affect both U.S. and Soviet capabilities and the regional balance of their forces.

7. Middle East military facilities under the control of the United States and the USSR are related by Arab media both to U.S. and Soviet regional capabilities and to the force balance.

8. Deployments, exercises, and maneuvers of forces in non-crisis periods are not associated by Arab media to military readiness and therefore are not associated with the local U.S.-USSR balance. The contrary is true during crisis periods.

9. Superpower airlift-sealift capabilities are seen to directly affect the local superpower balance.

10. The Arab press accepts that the United States and the Soviet Union are in a position of global strategic standoff. They do not follow the details of new strategic-weapons developments but assume a mutual deterrence capability both globally and regionally.

TABLE 9. 2

Symbolic Force Events and
Local Superpower Military Capabilities

Type of Event	Number of Obser- vations	Aggregate Space (cm^2)	Having an Effect			
			Obs.	Per- cent	(cm^2)	Per- cent
Visits	143	22,665	0	0	0	0
Games, maneuvers, exercises	40	2,401	0	0	0	0
Totals	183	25,066	0	0	0	0
Note: other deployments	155	16,547	1	0.6	586	3.5

Source: Compiled by author.

FINDINGS

1. Symbolic force events are not related by the media to the
local superpower balance or to the superpowers' local capabilities.
None of the 143 visits—which are symbolic force events—or
40 games, maneuvers, and exercises—many of which are also
symbolic events—was identified as having any effect on the regional
military balance between the United States and the Soviet Union. Only
two of the 155 other deployments were considered to influence the
balance. Thus, Table 9. 1 indicates that the Arab newspapers do not
equate symbolic force events for critical developments affecting the
balance.
      Similarly, symbolic force events are not perceived to have an
affect on local superpower military capabilities. Unlike the balance
issue, local capabilities could conceivably be affected by visits,
maneuvers, and the like. Nevertheless, none of the 143 visit observations or the 40 observations relating to maneuvers, games, and
exercises was stated by the newspapers to be likely to affect U. S.
or Soviet capabilities. Somewhat surprisingly, only one of the other
155 deployments was expected to have such an effect, according to
the newspapers (Table 9. 2).

TABLE 9.3

Attention to U.S. and Soviet Weapons
Performance and Technology

Country	Total Obser- vations	Total Space (cm^2)	Page 1 Articles	Banner Headlines	Major Headlines
U.S.	105	73,222	51 (47%)	43 (41%)	52 (50%)
USSR	59	16,267	29 (49%)	8 (14%)	34 (58%)
Superpowers	17	6,770	0 (0%)	2 (12%)	12 (71%)

Source: Compiled by author.

2. <u>U.S. weapons are generally considered superior in design and quality control to Soviet weapons of the same type. Exceptions are some SAM systems, ATGMs, and the Kalashnikov AK-47.</u>
The media do not seem to assume a consistent U.S. weapons superiority, but, in general, the United States is considered to enjoy an overall technology lead over the Soviet Union,[2] and this lead ramifies predictably on certain areas of complex weapons systems such as aircraft, in which even the MiG-23 is considered inferior to many Western aircraft.
However, in two areas—air-defense systems and ATGMs—the volume of newspaper data suggests Soviet weapons superiority. Although there is relatively little discussion of artillery, Soviet equipment was also considered superior in that field. Soviet SAMs received particularly abundant laudatory newspaper attention. Interestingly enough, the Arab press totally disregarded that Soviet SAM systems had a very low kill rate in the Yom Kippur war and that newer electronic countermeasures and better tactics later in the war further reduced SAM-inflicted Israeli aircraft losses (Tables 9.3 and 9.4).
3. <u>Foreign military missions are not considered as factors influencing either local superpower military capabilities or the regional balance between the United States and the USSR.</u>
Of the 25 observations addressing the subject of military missions, not one suggests any of the missions is likely to affect the military capabilities of either the United States or the USSR. In reality, however, the large-scale Soviet military training in Egypt did result in altering local Soviet military reconnaissance capabilities

TABLE 9.4

Media Attention to U.S. and Soviet Equipment,
(Weapons Performance and
Technology Subjects Only)
(Observations/cm^2)

Equipment Type	U.S.	USSR	Superpowers
Aircraft: combat	2/224	2/1185	1/310
Aircraft: other	1/288	1/2007	—
SAM	—	10/3813	—
SSM	—	2/620	—
SLBM	—	1/15	—
PGM	2/581	—	—
ATGM	—	2/250	1/470
Satellite	—	9/715	1/310
Nonlethal equipment	3/330	—	—

Source: Compiled by author.

to monitor the U.S. Sixth Fleet. Moreover, the availability of
Egyptian ports materially increased the flexibility of the Soviet
Mediterranean Squadron. Egyptian facilities supporting these activities,
while not technically a part of the mission's role, were provided in
exchange for the Soviet training effort. In this context, two of the
articles (8 percent) indicated that the military missions concerned
did affect the local superpower military balance.

4. The Arab press does not perceive a relationship between
weapons research and development (R&D) and the local military
balance or regional U.S. and Soviet military capabilities.

The media do not give credence to the importance of weapons
research with respect to the local force balance of the superpowers,
since none of the 149 relevant observations posited any such effect.
Counterintuitively, neither did the Arab newspapers have a single
observation dealing with weapons R&D that stated a likely impact
on the regional military capabilities of the United States and the
Soviet Union. We had expected coverage of Soviet naval carrier
procurement or construction of Western aircraft to demonstrate such
an effect. Weapons R & D events were seen to affect the military
balance between regional powers rarely (2.6 percent of the observations dealing with weapons development and performance), and the

TABLE 9. 5

Effect of RDT&E Time Lags

Action	Total Observations	No Time Lag				Time Lag			
		Observations	Effects			Observations	Effects		
			1[a]	2[b]	3[c]		1[a]	2[b]	3[c]
Test	177	174	—	—	5	3			—
Develop	35	25	—	—	2	10			1
Deploy	18	15	—	—	5	3			—
Produce	9	7	—	—	2	2			1
Other	77	69	—	—	1	8			—
Total	316	290	0	0	15	26	0	0	2

[a]Stated impact is on the local superpower force balance.
[b]Stated impact is on local superpower military capabilities.
[c]Stated impact is on the global military balance.
Source: Compiled by author.

global U. S. –USSR balance seldom (but less infrequently—12. 8 percent of the observations).

5. Arab media are not in a position to determine the time lags between research breakthrough and deployment. Consequently, these lags are not related by the Arab press to the local military balance between U. S. and Soviet forces.

With the recognition given time lag between weapons research, development, testing, and evaluation (RDT&E) and actual deployment, it is hardly surprising that.none of the observations in which time lags were considered suggested that the reported event would have an impact on the local force balance between the United States and the Soviet Union (Table 9. 5).

6. On the other hand, deployments of new systems are seen by the media to affect both American and Soviet capabilities and the regional balance of their forces.

New weapons systems deployed to local units of U. S. and Soviet military forces attract considerable media attention but are not perceived to have much effect. Of the 117 deployments of new weapons systems to superpower forces in the Middle East area, only one—less than one percent—was expected to affect the U. S. – Soviet regional balance (Table 9. 6).

TABLE 9. 6

New Systems Deployments and Effects

Weapons Systems	Number	Effects on Local Superpower	
		Balance	Capabilities
Major	62	0	0
Unknown	8	0	0
Other	47	1	0

Source: Compiled by author.

7. Middle East military facilities under the control of the United States and the USSR are related by Arab media both to U.S. and Soviet regional capabilities and to the force balance.

Bases in the Middle East are not seen to play a critical role in the local politicomilitary situation. Only 1.25 percent of the 160 bases observations indicated that the event would affect the local military balance of the superpowers, and none of the observations on this subject projected an impact on the military capabilities of the United States and the USSR in the Middle East-Persian Gulf area.

8. Deployments, exercises, and maneuvers of forces in non-crisis periods are not associated by Arab media with the local U.S.-USSR balance. The contrary is true during crisis periods.

Surprisingly, exercises and maneuvers do not seem to attract much more attention in crisis than in noncrisis periods. They receive slightly more space in noncrisis periods (61.2 cm^2 to 51.6 cm^2) and are almost three times as frequently covered (Table 9.7). Although the relative rarity of crises (even in the Middle East) is greater than this, one must consider the fact that the articles were selected to focus on such periods as the June and October Wars.

However, crisis deployments clearly attract media attention. Almost 60 percent of the deployments recorded occurred during crisis periods. The size of these articles was 31 percent greater than that of noncrisis deployments.

As a whole, 51 percent of the observations were related to crisis, and 59 percent of the space was devoted to crisis-coincident observations. Predictably, also, while only 20 percent of the editorials on the subjects were written for crisis-related or crisis-coincident observations, 75 percent of the banner headlines on this

TABLE 9.7

Exercises, Maneuvers, and Deployments

Activity	Crisis		Non-Crisis	
	Observations	Space (cm^2)	Observations	Space (cm^2)
Exercises & Maneuvers	9	464	32	1,957
Deployments	90	10,749	63	5,758
Total	99	11,213	95	7,715

Source: Compiled by the author.

theme accompanied deployments and other movements during crisis.

Of the 95 noncrisis observations of force movements, 32 dealt with exercises and maneuvers. None of these observations was related by the media to the global or local superpower force balances.

Surprisingly, none of the 90 crisis-deployment observations was explicitly stated to have an expected effect on the military balances at the global level.

None of the 72 deployments of forces in the Middle East, Persian Gulf, or other nearby areas during crisis was perceived to affect the regional U. S. -USSR force balance. Surprisingly—and quite counterintuitively—one noncrisis observation was perceived to have such an effect (Table 9.8).

9. Superpower airlift-sealift capabilities are seen to directly affect the local balance between the United States and the USSR.

Activities dealing with airlift and sealift capabilities and operations in our data sample were expected by the media to affect only local military balances between regional states (8.2 percent of the 49 observations). Indeed, U. S. -USSR airlift-sealift was the second most important category in terms of perceived impact on the local military situation (principally, the Arab-Israeli conflict). It was surprising that the media did not address the importance of airlift-sealift capability in the global strategic balance, since Western media discuss the subject frequently, nor was any effect seen on the regional force balance of the superpowers.

10. The Arab press accepts that the United States and the Soviet Union are in a position of global strategic standoff. They do not follow

TABLE 9.8

Effects of Force Movements

Timing	Observations	Effects on Local Superpower Balance
Crisis–coincident	72	0
Non–crisis–coincident	49	1

Source: Compiled by author.

the details of new weapons developments, but assume a mutual deterrence capability both globally and regionally.

The analysis of Arab newspapers suggests that this hypothesis is valid. We have elsewhere written of this perception of global strategic standoff and its implications. [3] We found no suggestion that any newspaper saw either superpower as having a decisive edge in military capabilities. Substantial awareness of, and interest in, events that are viewed as affecting the local balances of power among Arab countries and between the Arab states and Israel are not reflected in local superpower capabilities or in the regional global balance of U.S. and Soviet forces. Table 9.9 demonstrates this limited concern.

Another way of viewing the small proportion of events expected to have an impact on the U.S.-USSR balance is to point out that only 15.2 percent of all events dealing with these subject areas were perceived as likely to have an effect on either the global or local superpower balance or regional military capabilities of the United States or Soviet Union. Meanwhile, over 11 percent of military-assistance-and-sales observations posited some influence on local military balances between regional states.

The different levels of effect suggest that conflict salience dictates perceived effect. Although Arab media pay some attention to weapons-systems developments and the like, many articles suggest that the Arabs see the global rivalry as balanced, at least in the sense of a deterrent level of assured mutual destruction. Local superpower capabilities and the local U.S.-USSR balance seem to have little salience because a local superpower conflict is expected to become a global one, and because the local U.S. and Soviet forces are seen to have symbolic ("trigger") rather than military importance in terms of their contribution to the local problems that preoccupy elite

TABLE 9.9

Events Perceived to Affect
the Superpower Strategic Balance

Theme	Obser-vations	Local Superpower Balance		Local Superpower Capabilities		Global Balance	
		Obser-vations	Per-cent	Obser-vations	Per-cent	Obser-vations	Per-cent
U.S.-USSR strategic competition	198	2	1.0	2	1.0	60	30.3
Weapons development/ performance	149	0	0.0	0	0.0	19	12.8
Technological breakthroughs	167	0	0.0	0	0.0	2	1.2
Airlift/sealift	49	0	0.0	0	0.0	0	0.0
Total	563	2	0.4	2	0.4	81	14.4

Source: Compiled by author.

analysts. In other words, the U.S.-USSR military equation is simply not viewed as a local balance, and both forces are seen to have already the level of capabilities necessary to accomplish regional functions, including the deterring of the other from intervention. By contrast, many events are seen to affect the local balance among regional countries and the global U.S.-USSR balance.

CONCLUSIONS

The Arab media are not very attentive to the details of the U.S.-USSR military balance in the Middle East. The impact of deployments of personnel and weapons, of weapon technology developments, of security assistance and military sales, and of airlift and sealift capability, for example, is not believed to significantly alter or affect the regional superpower balance or even the capabilities of local U.S. or Soviet forces. The inattentiveness

suggests that the Arabs do not focus on regional power, probably
because they feel each superpower's forces deter the forces of the
other from intervention in the Middle East.

We are left with the ambivalent observation that, although the
individual elements contributing to or detracting from U.S. and Soviet
local power are not important to the regional audiences both Washington and Moscow seek to influence, the aggregate of regional power—
credible deterrence through symbolic presence—is vitally important
to them. Hence, the psychological elements of credibility may be
far more critical in their influence than factors concerning military
readiness.

NOTES

1. The codebook gives a thorough explanation of procedures
and requirements: Edward E. Azar, Suhaila Haddad, and R. D.
McLaurin, The Assessment of the Impact of Military Force: Codebook for the Force Assessment Content/Events Data System (FACES)
(Alexandria, Va.: Abbott Associates, Inc., 1976).

2. See R. D. McLaurin, "The Soviet-American Strategic
Balance: Arab Elite Views," International Interactions, III, no. 3
(1977): 236-37.

3. R. D. McLaurin with Suhaila Haddad, The Political Impact
of U.S. Military Force in the Middle East (Washington, D.C.:
American Institutes for Research, 1977), Chapter 5.

PART
3

CONCLUSION

10

ISSUES AND FINDINGS

Donald C. Daniel

This chapter highlights and draws together findings on issues addressed in two or more chapters of part two. While all the conclusions are subject to further investigation and refinement, they provide initial insights and can be useful when formulating hypotheses in future studies.

Issue one. Based on the most recent trend in each study, which state was viewed as ahead in overall military or strategic nuclear strength?

Agreement was not entirely uniform for either balance. On the one hand, a majority of British, French, and West German public opinion believed the Soviet Union to be equal to, or ahead of, the United States in total military strength with the greater bulk of this majority leaning toward Soviet superiority. The Japanese elite, on the other, perceived the Americans in possession of a very narrow lead. In the overall strategic-nuclear area, the Americans who expressed an opinion differed on the standing of the superpowers, but the Soviets, the Défense Nationale writers, and the Arabs generally characterized them as equal, with many of the last two groups believing it moot to ask, "Who is ahead?" in a situation of mutual nuclear overkill. These individuals saw the superpowers as functionally equal regardless of which had the quantitative or qualitative advantage.

Issue two: How did the superpowers compare in other military balances covered by the studies if one again focuses on the most recent trend?

It is difficult to generalize from the findings. The United States on the whole fared better than the Soviet Union, but the significance of its so doing is by no means clear. It was generally accepted as the leader in tactical nuclear weapons by the Japanese elite, in military technology by the Japanese and the Arabs, and in strategic bombs and warheads, ballistic-missile submarines, and strategic aviation by the French journal (i. e. , Défense Nationale) authors. These last also rated it superior or equal in naval power and equal to the Soviet Union in strategic missiles.

As for the regional superpower balance in the Middle East, the Arabs saw the Soviets and Americans as having more than enough power to do whatever they wanted militarily in the region. It mattered little to them which country was ahead at any point in time in regional strength. They also felt one could not decouple the local balance from the global balance; that is, strategic parity sets limits on whatever one superpower can do in the region in the face of opposition from the other.

Unfortunately, findings on U. S. –USSR conventional-or-ground-forces strengths are not available, but there is information on the NATO-Warsaw Pact balance in Europe. The Soviets asserted that alliance forces are essentially equal, a view which contrasts sharply with the unanimous opinion of Défense Nationale authors that the Soviet bloc is superior.

Issue three: Have recent shifts in perceived strength favored the United States or the Soviet Union?

These consistently favored the Soviet Union. This conclusion applies to Soviet, British, French, West German, Japanese, and, for the most part, U. S. views of the overall military or strategic nuclear balances, Japanese elite views of the military-technological balance, the French journal characterizations of the strategic missile and naval balances.

Issue four: How were the United States and Soviet Union rated in overall power (consisting of economic, political, and scientific, as well as military factors)?

The United States was perceived as superior by British, French, and West German public opinion as well as by the Japanese elite, but not by the Soviets, who felt that the "correlation of world forces" (which includes additional factors such as the ideological) had shifted in 1969 or 1970 to where they were now equal. Soviet spokesmen did acknowledge that the most significant factor affecting the change in the overall correlation was achievement of strategic parity. One implication is that they weighed the military-strategic factor more heavily than did the British, French, Germans, or Japanese, who seem in turn to have given more weight to economics.

Issue five: Did the United States' Western European and Japanese allies consistently prefer U. S. strategic-nuclear superiority?

The case studies dealing with British, French, and West German public opinion and with Japanese elite views suggest a relatively recent trend in which these observers prefer superpower strategic-nuclear equality rather than U. S. superiority. This trend seems associated with the belief that international stability is thereby enhanced.

Issue six: What were the perceived prospects of superpower conflict?

The prospects were assessed as low by U. S. spokesmen, Western European and Japanese elites, and, by implication, the Arabs. The Soviets also saw the prospects of war decreasing due to strategic equality which would cause "sober-minded" circles in the United States to realize the futility of war.

Issue seven: What was the perceived relation between the global strategic balance and local or regional superpower balances?

Japanese and Arab observers viewed the global strategic nuclear balance as overriding the local or regional superpower balance. In their minds, the global balance set limits on superpower activities in regional areas. In the Japanese case, however, U. S. efforts to maintain the local balance were seen as important indicators of U. S. resolve to stand up to the Soviets.

Preferences for strategic-nuclear equality by the British, French, and West German publics, on the assumption that stability was thereby enhanced, imply that they also may have seen "strategic override" applying to their regions. Many of the Défense Nationale authors seemed to be as sensitive as the Japanese about maintaining a local balance when they recommended that, with the advent of strategic equality, the Western alliance should increase its flexible-response capabilities.

Issue eight: Which sources (or categories of sources) were most prominently relied on by observers seeking information about superpower military capabilities?

Based on the Soviet, Défense Nationale, and Japanese analyses, it is clear that U. S. spokesmen and publications, followed by annuals describing national military forces (especially the IISS's Military Balance and the Jane's series), played pivotal roles in shaping perceptions. It is worth noting that the high reliance on U. S. sources did not necessarily lead to perceptions favoring the United States. The tendency of many U. S. spokesmen (particularly government officials at budget time) to emphasize Soviet strengths and U. S. weaknesses often had a negative impact on the perceived U. S. standing.

Issue nine: Do space exploits, military demonstrations, games, maneuvers, or deployments influence balance perceptions?

This is a very complex issue, and available evidence suggests the impact of such activities is uncertain. Events such as military visits, exercises, and deployments, even in crises, attracted much Arab media attention but did not elicit a reaction about the local superpower balance. In the case of the Japanese elite, the evidence was contradictory, but it was emphasized that the steady growth and geographic advances of Soviet naval forces and their conduct of large naval exercises such as the 1975 OKEAN maneuvers did contribute to Japanese misgivings about trends in the military balance. U. S. Seventh Fleet deployments to the Western Pacific and U. S. willingness to station troops in Korea were important for allaying such misgivings.

Issue ten: To what extent did the perceivers tend to think in terms of numerical comparisons of superpower military strength?

The USSR study indicates that the Soviets avoid numerical comparisons as a matter of course. In contrast, French journal authors relied on them over 40 percent of the time if one discounts the overall strategic-nuclear and conventional-or-ground-forces balances. The low reliance on quantitative measures for the former balance reflects the oft-stated French belief (shared by some U. S. and Soviet spokesmen) that overall strategic inventory totals have lost their significance due to the "balance of terror." It is generally felt that both sides have more than enough.

Issue eleven: Was any connection evident between views of the balance and willingness to support defense spending or efforts to increase military capabilities?

The findings on this issue suggest a connection. It is clear that the Soviets are very pleased to be accepted as the military and strategic equal of the United States. They are also pleased with the impact, as they see it, of this equality on aspects of U. S. foreign and military policy—particularly U. S. willingness to accept the Soviet Union as a coequal world actor and U. S. caution on issues which could lead to confrontation. As a consequence, they seem determined to do what is necessary to insure that the Soviet Union remains at least equal. Indeed, while some Soviet spokesmen question the value of seeking superiority in the face of assured mutual destruction, the official line remains that superiority is desirable for assuring deterrence of "imperialist adventures."

As for the U. S. spokesmen, those viewing strategic trends as unfavorable urged U. S. efforts to insure equality while their more confident colleagues, that is, those perceiving assured mutual

destruction, cautioned against overconcentration on maintaining
strict weapons parity. They feared that such concentration would be
at the expense of other important areas affecting U. S. security
ranging from nuclear terrorism to Third World needs.

Coincident with perceived superpower strategic equality, many
French journal authors encouraged France or Western Europe to
develop a force de frappe. Some encouraged the NATO alliance to
increase its flexible-response capability. The force de frappe
recommendations were linked to one or two beliefs. The first was
that, with parity, France or Western Europe could no longer rely
on the U. S. nuclear umbrella. The second was that the commanding
lead held jointly by both the United States and Soviet Union in strategic
power could result in a superpower condominium, a situation to
be obviated by development of French or Western European nuclear
capabilities. The flexible response recommendation reflected the
obvious concern that, in a situation of nuclear standoff, the Western
alliance had to be better prepared to meet threats at lower levels.

While uneasy about military and strategic trends, the Japanese
elite felt themselves powerless to do much about it, but they did
want the United States to continue to play a balancing role. Their
fear was that U. S. resolve to insure military and strategic equality
was in a period of relative decline.

Finally, the case study of British, French, and West German
public opinion addressed this issue in a slightly different manner.
Focusing on the "defense burden" (defense budget/gross domestic
product) of each state over time, the study concluded that, except
for Germany, as the United States' perceived position in the military
balance improved, national defense burdens decreased.

Issue twelve: Did recent perceived shifts in some balances away
from U. S. favor result in recommendations that accommodations
with the Soviets should be sought.

Even though many French authors perceived some trends as
unfavorable to the United States, none recommended that France
should, as a result, increase its ties with the Soviet Union. The
same conclusion generally, but not totally, applies to the Japanese
elite. While as a whole it favored continued maintenance of the U. S.
alliance, there was incipient support among some members for
supplemental security guarantees involving the USSR. Interestingly
enough, Soviet observers felt that the Americans did move toward
closer accommodation with the onset of strategic parity, and
recommendations by some U. S. spokesmen supporting the SALT
process help provide confirmation for the Soviet views.

In conclusion, it is hoped that others will build upon the above
findings, confirming, modifying, or adding to them as appropriate.

One area which particularly needs more explicit attention is the perceived strength of the willingness of the superpowers to play a balancing role. As already noted, Japanese elite observers were concerned that U. S. resolve to match Soviet military strength was in decline. Should many observers feel that way, the end result would be very significant for the United States, whatever its actual or perceived physical strength compared with the Soviet Union.

INDEX

ABMs, 160
ACDA (Arms Control and Disarmament Agency), 66
Africa, 163, 165
al-Ahram, 170
al-Hayat, 170
Allison, Lt. Gen. Royal, 63-64
analysis: content, 104, 114, 171; contextual, 135; factor, 41; multiple-regression, 117-21, 123; perceptual-impact, 36-38; regression, 100-101, [by ordinary least-squares (OLS) regression, 101]; trend, 99, 100, 102; time-series, 109
Angolan war, 89
an-Nahar, 170
Annual Defense Department Reports, 97
Arab perceptions of Mideast superpower regional balance, 170-81; data covered in study, 170-71; hypotheses used in study, 171-72; study findings, 173-81, [airlift-sealift abilities only affect local situations, 178; exercises and maneuvers attention-getters but without impact, 177-78; foreign military missions not factors of influence, 174-75; military bases not significant, 177; new weapons systems of little effect, 176; R&D of no importance to balance, 175-76; symbolic force events not related to local balance, 173; time lag before weapons deployment of

no importance, 176; U.S. weapons, with exceptions, held superior, 174; U.S.-USSR standoff accepted as fact, 178-80]
Arab-Israeli wars, 178; June War, 171, 173; (1973), 89; Yom Kippur War, 171, 174, 177
Arbatov, Georgi, 97-98
Armed Forces of the Soviet State, The, 85-86
arms control, 58, 60, 67
Arms Control Association, 59
ash-Sharq, 170
Asia, 153, 154
Aspen Institute Program in Communication and Society, 62
ASW (antisubmarine warfare), 43
ATGMs (antitank guided missiles), 171, 174
Australia, 30
Austria, 24, 73
autocorrelation, 100, 101
Azar, E., 114

Backfire bombers, 37, 60
Berlin, 24
Berlin crisis (1958), 73, 109, 121
B-52 bombers, 21
B-1 bombers, 36, 81
Bolshevik Revolution, 75
Brazil, 31
Brezhnev, Leonid, 76, 79, 80, 82
Brookings Institution, 159
Brown, Harold, 67, 85

Carter, President Jimmy, 67, 83
Center for Defense Information, 62

multiple-attribute utility (MAU)
measurements, 40, 42-52;
assessment of, 48-50; problems remaining in, 51-52

Nasser, Gamal Abdel, 131
National Security Council, 65
national will, 9, 59, 70, 165, 189
NATO, 9-10, 16, 23, 25-26, 30,
36, 37, 66, 81, 83, 87, 114,
130, 131, 134, 135, 147, 148,
186, 189
Nazi Germany, 75
Neal, Fred Warner, 60
neutron bombs, 81
new weapons, development of,
59, 66, 81
New York Times, 159
1970 Jordanian crisis, 171
Nitze, Paul, 58, 60
Nixon, President Richard M.,
77, 79, 159
Nixon doctrine, 159, 163
North Korea, 30, 47, 48, 157
Nuclear Nonproliferation Treaty,
171
nuclear umbrella, U.S., 189

objective tension, 114
oil embargo (1973), 96
OKEAN II (1975), 174, 166, 188
Oman, 170
ordinary least-squares (OLS)
regression, 101
overall conclusions of study: its
balancing role, retention of,
favored by U.S.'s allies, 189;
exercises and
unimportant to Arabs, less so
to Japanese, 188; French
force de frappe encouraged,
189; global balance seen more
important than for regional
areas, 187; information
sources primarily U.S., 187;
military-nuclear superiority,

no clear opinion on, 185; new
accommodations with Soviets,
little seeking for, 189; other
military balances, opinions
varied on, 185-86; for overall
power, U.S. favored by all but
Soviets, 186; quantitative arms
balances no longer significant,
188; recent shifts in strength
toward USSR, 186; Soviets still
seeking greater superiority,
188; strategic-nuclear parity
preferred by U.S. allies, 187;
superpower conflict, little
prospect of, 187

Pakistan, 48
perceivers: classes of, 11-12, 30;
studies of, 12-13; by types of
national systems, 30-31
perception, modalities of, 30-34;
by classes of perceivers, 30,
31-32; by types of national
systems, 30-31
perceptions, impact of, 17-19;
historical examples, 18; Soviet
use of, 19; U.S. and, 19
perceptions, reality in, 15-17;
deviations from, 15-17, [lead
and lag hypotheses, 16-17]
perceptions, sources of, 13-15;
credibility of, 15
perceptions of the military balance,
characteristics of, 3-7; affect,
5-6; definition, 3; direction
and rate of change, 6; relation
to reality, 6-7; stability, 5
perceptual impact of information,
32-34
perceptual-impact analyses, 36-
38
Peru, 48
political utility of armed forces,
24-25, 28-30
Pravda, 159
PRC (see China, People's Republic of)

ABOUT THE EDITORS
AND CONTRIBUTORS

DONALD C. DANIEL teaches in the Department of National
Security Affairs of the Naval Postgraduate School, Monterey,
California. He has a Ph. D. in Political Science from Georgetown
University and is the author of several articles on naval and maritime
affairs.

MICHAEL J. DEANE is a research assistant professor at the
Center for Advanced International Studies, University of Miami,
Coral Gables, Florida. He is a former research analyst (1974-76)
at the Strategic Studies Center, Stanford Research Institute. He
received his doctorate in International Affairs from the University
of Miami in 1974. His major areas of research have focused on
Soviet foreign policy and Soviet military affairs. His most recent
publication is Political Control of the Soviet Armed Forces.

HERBERT GOLDHAMER was a RAND Corporation analyst in
Santa Monica, California. He was the author of several books, his
most recent being The Soviet Soldier and the Adviser. He passed
away on August 8, 1977.

PAUL LANGER is a senior staff member of the Social Science
Department of the RAND Corporation in Santa Monica, California. He
has written extensively on Far Eastern affairs and international
relations. He is the coauthor of North Vietnam and the Pathet Lao.

EDWARD J. LAURANCE is an Associate Professor at the Naval
Postgraduate School in Monterey, California. He teaches in the
Department of National Security Affairs and specializes in arms-
transfer research. He holds a Ph. D. in Political Science from the
University of Pennsylvania.

EDWARD N. LUTTWAK is a visiting professor in the Department
of Political Science of the Johns Hopkins University, Baltimore,
Maryland, and the author of The US-USSR Nuclear Weapons Balance,
The Dictionary of Modern War, and The Political Uses of Sea Power.

ROBERT B. MAHONEY, JR., is the manager of the Projections
and Plans Department, CACI, Inc.-FEDERAL. His research interests
include the political uses of military force, the influences of

psychological factors in interstate relations, and modeling and simulation. He holds a Ph. D. in Political Science from Northwestern University.

R. D. MCLAURIN is a senior staff member of Abbott Associates, Inc. , Alexandria, Virginia. He was previously with the American Institutes for Research and the Office of the Secretary of Defense. Dr. McLaurin is the author of The Middle East on Soviet Policy, co-author of Foreign Policy Making in the Middle East, and coeditor of The Art and Science of Psychological Operations.

RONALD G. SHERWIN is an assistant professor of political science at the Naval Postgraduate School, Monterey, California. He specializes in events data analysis and is involved in a major arms-transfer research project. He has a Ph. D. from the University of Southern California.

RELATED TITLES
Published by Praeger Special Studies

ARMS CONTROL AND EUROPEAN SECURITY:
A Guide to East-West Negotiations

> Joseph I. Coffey

CURRENT ISSUES IN U. S. DEFENSE POLICY

> Center for Defense Information
> edited by
> David T. Johnson
> Barry R. Schneider

THE ESTIMATION OF SOVIET DEFENSE
EXPENDITURES, 1955-75; An Unconventional
Approach

> William T. Lee

THE MILITARY IN CONTEMPORARY SOVIET
POLITICS: An Institutional Analysis

> Edward L. Warner III

SOVIET NAVAL INFLUENCE: Domestic and
Foreign Dimensions

> edited by
> Michael MccGwire
> John McDonnell